W9-CSZ-375

"How do you go deeper, dream bigger, and live with more intention when your kids won't even leave you alone in the bathroom? That's a challenge facing most young moms today, which is why I so appreciate Jenny's new book. Not only has Jenny written in a bite-sized, accessible format for moms-on-the-go, but her book is full of wisdom, advice, and challenges for women who crave more. You don't have to settle for surviving this season of life. You can live with great intention, and this book will get you started!"

— **Sharon Hodde Miller,** regular contributor to *Her.meneutics* and blogger at SheWorships.com

"The early years of motherhood are so difficult! On one hand, we adore our new role as mommy. On the other hand, we may feel like the woman we once were—a woman with God-given leadership gifts, callings, and passions—no longer exists or even matters. For any mom who has wrestled with that tension, Jenny Rae Armstrong comes alongside you like a girlfriend who 'gets it.' With humor, practicality, and wisdom, she encourages and equips you to powerfully serve God and to make a difference in the world—from right where you are."

— **Aubrey Sampson,** author, *Overcomer: Breaking Down the Walls of Shame and Rebuilding Your Soul*

"Wise and witty Jenny Rae Armstrong has created the most realistic and guilt-free resource for families. Her book will equip your children to think beyond the front door. Armstrong demonstrates that age means precious little when it comes to serving neighbors and beyond. She teaches from experience with a huge heart and great humility, even incorporating a plethora of ideas from parents worldwide. The suggestions will spark creativity to help you and your family discover unique ways to serve others. I highly recommend this book to any parent who longs to live out the gospel of Jesus Christ while needing to also do the laundry, cook dinner, and drive carpools."

— **Sharon R. Hoover,** Director of Missions, Centreville Presbyterian Church, Washington DC metro area

"Jenny Rae Armstrong beautifully answers the nagging question many of us ask, 'What can I do?' With humor, poignancy and accessible tips, this book helps us embrace the truth that joining with God in the work he is already doing around us is easier than we think."

— **Shayne Moore,** author, *Global Soccer Mom* and *Refuse to Do Nothing*

"Jenny paints a picture of real life interposed with the beauty of the divine moments of motherhood. With a twist of humor and relevance, she shows how the mundane activities of life can be meaningful and missional."

— **Lorie Lee,** CEO: Be Global in Your Local (beglobalinyourlocal.com)

"Where was this book when my kids were small and I needed some wisdom and light? The ideas and practices in this treasure-trove will bring beautiful illumination to parents raising children in the light of God's truths and love."

—**Leslie Leyland Fields,** author of *The Spirit of Food* and *Surviving the Island of Grace*

"Jenny has lit a bright light for mamas around the world in this book. Her words and stories expand our values beyond imagination: the value of family and the value of the Kingdom of God; work and play; individuals and community; the church and the mission field; giving and caring. She shines a light on contributions mothers make not only to their families, but also to a world in need, all augmented with innovative ideas and practical opportunities. A life-changing read for any mom."

—**Judy Douglass,** author and speaker, Director, Women's Resources, Office of the President, Campus Crusade for Christ/Cru

"*Don't Hide Your Light* is written by a mom to other moms who find it hard to even think about mission amid the daily challenges of changing diapers and going to soccer tournaments. I'm so glad I didn't just reflexively hand my copy to my wife or sister or daughter, and instead engaged it myself. Mother or not, official missionary or not, this delightfully written book will make you think and laugh on your way to understanding the essential truth that mission begins with me right where I am."

—**Al Tizon,** Executive Minister of Serve Globally, Evangelical Covenant Church, affiliate associate professor of Missional and Global Leadership, North Park Theological Seminary

"As a member of the Redbud Writers Guild, I have been impressed by Jenny Rae's thoughtful, pastoral approach to giving women a voice. That she would offer this resource as a megaphone for other women to tell their stories demonstrates a kind of pastoral attention and joyful generosity that makes me proud to call her a colleague."

—**Sarah Arthur,** author or editor of eleven books, including *The Year of Small Things: Radical Faith for the Rest of Us*

"Anyone who's raised kids knows that figuring out how to love God and live out your gifts along with the all-consuming needs of young kids is tough! Enter Jenny Rae Armstrong: her encouraging, down-to-earth writing will give you the strength you need to turn to God in all things— even when you are drowning in the laundry basket. If you are looking for straight talk about being a mother with a mission, Jenny Rae Armstrong has written a book for you!"

—**Nicole Unice,** pastor, mother, and author of *She's Got Issues* and *Brave Enough*

JENNY RAE ARMSTRONG

LEAFWOOD
PUBLISHERS
an imprint of Abilene Christian University Press

DON'T HIDE YOUR LIGHT UNDER A LAUNDRY BASKET
150 Bright Ideas for Wannabe World Changers

LEAFWOOD
P U B L I S H E R S
an imprint of Abilene Christian University Press

Copyright © 2016 by Jenny Rae Armstrong

ISBN 978-0-89112-391-0

Printed in the United States of America

Scripture quotations, unless otherwise noted, are from The Holy Bible, New International Version®, NIV®. Copyright © 1973, 1978, 1984, 2011 by Biblica, Inc.® Used by permission. All rights reserved worldwide.

Scripture quotations marked NLT are taken from the Holy Bible, New Living Translation, copyright © 1996, 2004, 2007 by Tyndale House Foundation. Used by permission of Tyndale House Publishers, Inc., Carol Stream, Illinois 60188. All rights reserved.

Scripture quotations noted KJV are taken from the King James Version of the Bible.

Published in association with Books & Such Literary Agency, 52 Mission Circle #122, PMB 170, Santa Rosa, CA 95409.

Cover design by ThinkPen Design, LLC
Interior text design by Sandy Armstrong, Strong Design

Leafwood Publishers is an imprint of Abilene Christian University Press
ACU Box 29138
Abilene, Texas 79699

1-877-816-4455
www.leafwoodpublishers.com

16 17 18 19 20 21 / 7 6 5 4 3 2 1

For my husband, Aaron.
Not every man is willing to take his wife's gifts, dreams,
and callings as seriously as his own, much less make the sacrifices
and put in the work to support her in them. You are an amazing
example of Christlike, selfless love; an encouragement to everyone
lucky enough to know you; and a rock star with a Crock-Pot.
Thank you. I love you.

ACKNOWLEDGMENTS

Writing a book is a lot of work, but living with a person who is writing a book may be even more challenging. Aaron, thank you for all the sacrifices you have made, all of the extra hours you put in at work and at home, to enable me to do this. Thank you for seeing things in me that I did not see in myself, and urging me to lean into them. Thank you for just being you. I love you.

To my sons, Jamison, Clay, Carter, and Grant—you guys are amazing, and I am so proud of you. Jamison, thanks for always springing into action when the chips are down—when, say, your brother breaks his arm while Mom and Dad are at a conference, or the pickle jar is really, really stuck. Clay, you are so nurturing—thanks for all the homemade treats and other ways you love on people. Carter, your creativity and energy bring so much to our family! Just thinking about you makes me smile. Grant, thanks for making my home office your reading nook of choice. I love hanging out with you!

Thanks so much to my father-in-law, Jack Armstrong, and mother-in-law, Karen Armstrong, for filling in the gaps with our kids when both Aaron and I had to work long hours. I love you both and appreciate you so much!

To my parents, Larry and Gail Williams: How can I even begin to thank you for the blessing you have been in my life? It's an impossible task! So, I'll just say thank you. Thanks for taking me swimming in the Atlantic and ice skating on the Amnicon. Thanks for waking me up to see the northern lights, and pointing out the beauty of African sunsets. Thanks for always telling me that I could be anything I wanted to be, and backing those words up with your full support. I am so thankful for both of you, and for the godly heritage you passed down to me.

When it comes to churches, there is no doubt that I have hit the ecclesial jackpot. Many thanks to the wonderful people of Mission Covenant Church in Poplar, Wisconsin, who have loved me and my family so well for generations. You *are* family, and I love you all to pieces. Thanks especially to Pastor Darrell Nelson, who mentored me for years and urged me to keep pressing forward in ministry, even when my knees were shaking. You may never know how much your encouragement strengthened me. Thanks to the people of Darrow Road Wesleyan Church, who welcomed me with open arms—literally! Your hugs, your smiles, and your encouragement bless me every week. Thanks as well to the people of Salem Covenant Church in Duluth, Minnesota, and Faith United Methodist Church in Superior, Wisconsin. You have all been such blessings to me!

Speaking of the *ecclesia,* where would I be without the incredible women of the Redbud Writer's Guild? You are my people. I love "fearlessly expanding the feminine voice" with you!

Thanks to my agent Rachel Kent, who caught the vision for this funny little collection of essays and worked tirelessly to get it into the right hands. Thanks as well to the people at Leafwood Publishers who polished it up and made it shine. I am so thankful for all of your work!

CONTENTS

FOREWORD

"Someone's gotta go!"
My husband and I had just adopted our sweet son Abhishek from India. He was two years old. Our older son, Rollie, was two and a half. Our daughter, Zoe, was four.

And just weeks into being the parent of three, I was losing my marbles.

"I don't care if you apply to grad school or get a job, but some-one's gotta go!"

The confused looks on my children's faces snapped me back into reality. Taking a deep breath, I could admit that small people who would prefer to go without clothes should probably not be admitted into a PhD program or garner a paycheck. Also, each one needed their mommy during most waking moments.

So it wasn't my finest mothering moment.

Like a lot of moms, I was frustrated.

It wasn't just the daily driveway carjackings of ride-on toys, the preparation of endless healthy-ish finger-food meals, or the squab-bles over whose day it was to manage Thomas the Tank Engine at the tabletop rail yard. Like a lot of moms, I missed the life I once lived.

As a single young adult, I'd been privileged to respond to God's call to engage with a world in need in the most satisfying ways. With other college students, I built relationships with folks who lived outdoors in downtown Santa Barbara, California. I joined five hundred others on an annual mission trip to Mexico, where we served under local pastors and congregations. I walked through occupied South African townships during apartheid, when Nelson Mandela was still imprisoned on Robben Island. I ran an after-school program in the New Jersey city dubbed "America's Most Dangerous City." Before my Zoe was born, I served as a director of spiritual development to people who lived with physical and intellectual disabilities.

For a girl who was itchy to adventure with Jesus, it really didn't get any better than my awesome life.

So changing diapers 24/7 felt like quite a demotion.

I understood, though, what a privilege it was to have the opportunity to be at home with my kiddos. And I even believed the campaign that insisted to weary mamas like me, "Being a mom is the most important job in the world!"

So why wasn't I more satisfied?

It's because I'd been made for so much more. We all have.

Though I didn't know exactly what it should look like, I became convinced that moms were called to *more* than meeting the physical, emotional, intellectual, and spiritual needs of our own charges. To *more* than filling our children's waking hours with visits to playgrounds, museums, and zoos. To *more* than watching endless hours of Arthur cartoons.

Though I couldn't have known it then, what I really needed was *Don't Hide Your Light under a Laundry Basket*. But even without such a lifeline, God was faithful to show me how I could shine my light right where I was. (Though the lessons weren't delivered half as delightfully as they are in this book.)

My family started sponsoring Joshua, a boy in India just the age of my boys, through Compassion International so that his physical, emotional, intellectual, and spiritual needs would be met.

We packed the car with snacks we could share, on our way to the zoo, with the guy on the side of the road who was hungry. We read a book together about a little girl whose old Grandma finally got to vote in the first South African elections that were open to all citizens. In the mundane moments of our days, we discovered ways to love God and love people.

I continue to be convinced that God's love and plan for a world in need can never be pulled apart from God's love and plan for mamas who are raising kids. Rather, God gives us opportunities to love the ones God loves at the grocery store, at the swimming pool, and beside tiny peewee-size soccer fields.

Beloved sisters, this is what you're made for. And in Jenny Rae Armstrong, you have a guide who is a neighbor-lovin' genius. She knows what your dirty-dish, unfolded-laundry life is like, and in these pages she's gifting you with practical ways to follow Jesus right where you are, alongside the amazing little creatures you're with every day.

This is the book I wanted and needed. And I pray that it will encourage and inspire you to keep being the woman, and the mama, God created you to be.

Margot Starbuck
Author of *Small Things with Great Love:
Adventures in Loving Your Neighbor*

INTRODUCTION

"I feel like I've been benched." Jen shifted the baby on her hip and brushed the bangs of her pixie cut out of her eyes, scanning the campground for her kids as she updated me on her life. "God's given me this big vision, but with a baby, a two-year-old, and home-schooling Nate, it's like all I do is wash laundry and clean spit-up. I know this vision is for the long term, and I don't want to wish away these years with my kids, but it's hard."

I could empathize. After all, it had only been two years since we had shared a midnight in the sacred sanctuary of the campground's women's bathroom, praying about the callings weighing heavily on our hearts. But Jen's oldest was the age of my youngest, and those two years had highlighted the difference in our phases of life. My oldest was in high school now, and my baby had started elementary school, freeing me up to do more with my writing, take a position at my church, and even pursue my longtime dream of going to seminary. But Jen's growing family rooted her more and more firmly in Diapersville, in those exhausting, exhilarating years when only your pinched budget and hormone-induced adoration of your babies keep you from running off to Cancun to sleep away a month of Sundays.

I forced down the platitudes—"it's only a phase" and "you'll never regret the time you spend with your babies"—and scooted over to offer her and Baby Annabelle the shady spot on the lawn swing.

"That is hard," I agreed. "They're great years, but hard."

Can we just admit that those early years of child-rearing are hard? Sure, we wouldn't trade those toothless baby grins for anything, and seeing our rough-and-tumble first grader suck his thumb in his sleep is enough to break our hearts with love. But the isolation, exhaustion, and lost sense of purpose so many of us experience during those years can suck the life right out of us. I mean, really? We spent fifty thousand dollars and four years in college for this? To break up fights over plastic dinosaurs and clean up after the baby's hilarious "let's throw the peas on the floor" game?

The messages we get from the world around us aren't much help either. Either we're supposed to be a manic Pinterest mom—completely fulfilled in our domestic duties of baking cake pops, stenciling glittery Bible verses on our daughter's bedroom wall, and playing Candyland for the ten billionth time—or we're supposed to sell all our earthly possessions, become house parents at an orphanage in Haiti, and wear nothing but tank tops, maxi skirts, and overpriced Toms for the rest of our lives. Seriously, there is not enough coffee in the world, and after giving birth to four strapping boys, I don't have the body for tank tops and maxi skirts anymore.

There is no question that there's great value in child-rearing, in molding young minds, and creating a nurturing home for your family. At the same time, there's a big world beyond the walls of our homes, crying out for the healing and redemption we're called to offer in the name of Christ. Who says we can't do both? We may need to flex and flow a little bit, keep an emergency stash of Cheerios in our purses, and arrange our schedules around naptimes. But in the long run, our kids will come out better for it. When children see their mothers serve, and are able to serve alongside

them, they realize that they are not, in fact, the center of the universe. That we are all blessed to be a blessing to others.

So this book is for the mommies: for the artist who spends hours decorating Elmo cupcakes; for the superhero who has to pack two diaper bags, one backpack, and four different lunches before rushing off to work; and for that crazy (but svelte) woman who sprints down the side of the road every morning, pushing her babies ahead of her in a double-wide jogging stroller. There is no guilt or shame here, just ideas to spark your creativity and help you come up with creative ways to make your unique contribution to God's kingdom. After all, we mommies know that few things delight a child's heart more than working alongside their parents and feeling that they have made a contribution. Our heavenly father has invited us to pull up a stool and help him cook up his plans for this world. Let's roll up our sleeves and plunge our hands into the mix!

POWER OUTLET ONE

Soul Care for Mamas on a Mission

Remember that old song by Sister Hazel? "If you wanna be somebody else, change your mind."[1] Yeah, I know, you were probably rocking out to it on the school bus while I was shuttling my firstborn to speech therapy. But it's an awesome song, and not a bad representation of what Jesus does in our hearts and minds when we decide to go all in for him.

I'm going to level with you: I was worried about writing this book, worried that you might see it as some sanctified to-do list to add to your car-seat-weight load of mommy guilt. Nothing could be further from the truth! Listen up: if you are a postpartum mama from Nowheresville, Indiana, freaking out about how you're not volunteering at an urban soup kitchen, dishing up Tater Tot casserole with the baby strapped to your boobs, I want you to email me right now so I can talk you off the ledge. Seriously. You don't need one more thing to worry about. You need a month or so of uninterrupted sleep, and maybe Zoloft.

On the other hand, I remember what it's like to live with a sense of holy discontent. To feel like you've lost yourself in giving life to others, and grieve gifts and callings that seem to have gone dormant. If that's where you're at, I hope this book is a nice warm sun shower for the seedling in your soul. Grow, baby, grow!

Anyhow, back to Sister Hazel. Here's the thing you have to understand: as Christians, we don't just do good works because it's the right thing to do. If that's our motivation, we're nothing more than a clanging gong or a resounding cymbal, as the apostle Paul wrote in 1 Corinthians 13. No, our good works flow out of what God is doing in us and in the ways Jesus is changing our hearts and minds, enabling us to love.

That's right. Our good works flow from a heart transformed by love. Not guilt. Not obligation. Not fear or competition or insecurity. Love.

This section is all about how we can cooperate with God's construction work in our hearts and minds. I realize that many of you may want to skip ahead to the exciting stuff, and that's fine. Skip around all you want! Just make sure to come back to this section every once in a while. After all, the first step to changing the world is changing yourself, and the first step to changing yourself is allowing Jesus to change your mind.

Learn to Pray like the Early Church Prayed

I'm always in awe of people who love to pray. You know—the tiny old lady everyone calls with their problems because she's like the Rambo of prayer warriors, or the coworker who waxes rhapsodic about the word God gave them in their closet that morning. I envy that ease and connection, I'll admit. But how do they sit *still* that long?

I grew up in a family that prayed about everything from lost keys to lost souls, anytime, anywhere, out loud, and without preamble. Oh, we recited common childhood prayers before meals and bedtimes, but the general consensus was that talking to God was just like talking to your best friend, an ongoing conversation lived out in real time. And it's true! I am thankful for the incredible foundation they laid for me.

But the older I got, the less these on-the-go prayers satisfied me. I touched base with God throughout the day, but every time I sat down to pray, my mind would wander to something else. I tried keeping a list of things to pray about in my Bible, but wound up feeling like I was asking God to pop over to the grocery store for milk and tampons. I tried journaling my prayers, and while I enjoyed that, I eventually realized that the only thing distinguishing my prayer journal from the diaries I kept as a teenager were the issues I complained about and the conspicuous lack of doodled hearts. Sometimes, if no one was around, I'd pull up a chair for Jesus and just start talking to him. But that's tough to explain to some adults, much less my autistic preschooler.

Long story short, I was crazy about God, but I felt guilty and defeated about my anemic prayer life.

Then one Sunday, my pastor preached a sermon on the Lord's Prayer. He explained that Jews in Jesus' day recited common prayers at fixed hours of the day, a tradition the early church carried on, and that many churches still practice today. I had one of those Hollywood epiphanies, where the heroine stares enraptured at the sky as light breaks through the clouds and angelic choruses play on a cheap synthesizer. I didn't have to rely on my limited creativity, scattered brainpower, and short attention span to build a meaningful prayer life. There was a rich tradition of common prayer that I could draw upon: prayers carefully composed by the psalmists, by heroes of the faith, and by Jesus himself that I could use to express my heart to God when my own words failed.

This doesn't mean that my prayer life has been all sunshine and roses since. I grew up wary of rote prayers and "vain repetitions" (as if we were more spiritual than the Lutherans down the street because we made up our own prayers), so the first several times I opened up *The Book of Common Prayer*, I couldn't figure out how to use it. I needed *Prayer for Dummies*, or a confirmation class, or something! But I muddled through, and was thrilled to discover that for the most part, it was just Scripture strung together to lead you deeper into prayer, worship, and reflection. Like *Our Daily Bread*, only written by people like King David and Mary and the apostle Paul instead of Guy Everyman from Ourtown, USA. And bonus: not only did these scriptural prayers leave me pondering their meaty themes all day, they often served as a springboard for my own spontaneous prayers.

You don't have to buy a prayer book to do this. Try reciting the Lord's Prayer every morning, really thinking through the words. Add a Psalm to your daily reading, making the psalmist's prayer your own. There are common prayer apps for your phone;

download one and try it out for a while. If you want to tackle a prayer book, you can download the public domain versions of the *Book of Common Prayer* free online, or check out a prayer book written for beginners, like *The Divine Hours* by Phyllis Tickle. Who knows? It may be just what your prayer life needs to go from frustrating to fruitful.

Keep a Gratitude Journal

When I was a little girl, back in the dark ages before drum sets and electric guitars were common in churches, my Grandma Irma played the organ at evening services at our church. People could call out the number of the hymn they wanted to sing, and my grandmother's pantyhose-clad feet would polka across the organ pedals. Sometimes, if we were really mixing it up, she would whip out her accordion and play the hymn old-world style. I particularly remember a catchy little turn-of-the-century tune we used to sing that had this chorus: "Count your blessings, name them one by one. Count your many blessings; see what God has done."[2]

I am so grateful for my vivacious, fun-loving grandmother and the wonderful memories I have of her! She was one of my best blessings.

Motherhood can be exhausting. Some days feel like a grind, a never-ending series of tantrums, bodily fluid malfunctions, and menial tasks that never stay done. It's on those days we need a little perspective, and keeping a gratitude journal is a great way to foster it.

Grab a scrap of paper, or an old notebook, or that pretty journal you got for Christmas and have been saving for a special purpose. It doesn't really matter, as long as you'll be able to find it later. You can ease into gratitude journaling by writing things that you are generally thankful for (Sunshine! Chocolate! Yoga pants that masquerade as work pants!), but try keeping a page for the people you interact with on a regular basis. Keeping a list of your tween's best characteristics, or remembering the sticky, wilted dandelions your preschooler picked for you the other day, will help you keep your cool when the afternoon goes south. Pondering the things you appreciate about your spouse (even if you have to think really, really hard some days) is one of the best gifts you can give your family. Remembering how your mom always made pancakes on the first day of school and how your father took you prom dress shopping at the mall may salve some hurts in your relationship with them. And don't stop with your family members; let your pastors, and next door neighbors, and your kids' teachers in on the love too. With the exception of dangerous or abusive people, if you know someone well enough to get legitimately mad at them, you should know them well enough to be grateful for them too.

If you want to take your gratitude journal to the next level, try making it public! Put a note in your child's lunch, telling them something you like about them. Make a list of things you appreciate about your husband, and leave it on his pillow. Pop a heartfelt card in your pastor's mailbox, or pick up the phone and call that favorite aunt you only see a couple times a year. One thing my family does on a regular basis is have everyone say one thing they appreciate about a given family member (no sarcasm, passive aggression, or veiled insults allowed), and then move on to the next person, until everyone has been complimented by every member of the family. It sounds corny, but it is incredibly meaningful. We all need a little encouragement sometimes.

Count your blessings. Name them one by one. And it will surprise you what the Lord has done![3]

Find Your Tribe

> "You are the average of the five people
> you spend the most time with."
>
> —Jim Rohn

I don't remember where I first heard that quote (although I've learned it's attributed to Jim Rohn, who was like the Tony Robbins of the 1970s), but it rocked my world. In fact, I would go so far as to say it changed my life. If Jim were still around, he'd probably be nodding smugly and trying to sell me an exorbitantly priced self-help course.

You know how your parents used to lecture you about choosing your friends wisely? It turns out they were right. The people we spend time with influence us, in positive and negative ways. Now I'm not saying that you should ditch your high-drama friends or only spend time with people who look, think, act, and believe just like you. How awful. I'm not a fan of the holy huddle mentality, particularly since Jesus was constantly pulling people in from the margins.

But if we are going to become the people God is calling us to be, we are going to need the guidance, encouragement, and ongoing support of people who are on that journey too—preferably a little further down the road than we are. And that doesn't necessarily happen by accident, particularly when a large percentage of the five people we spend the most time with wear diapers. We need to seek out mentors and friends who will help us get where we want to go.

For me, those mentors and friends are the incredible women of the Redbud Writer's Guild. I spent nearly a decade writing things only my husband and my mom were allowed to see, before working up the courage to submit anything for publication. I got a few articles published (which was absolutely thrilling), but the real transformation began when I was accepted into Redbud. It was intimidating at first—all these well-connected Wheatonites with their book contracts and advanced degrees, when I was a college dropout from the backwoods of Wisconsin, drowning in dirty diapers and regurgitated breast milk. But as I put aside my insecurities and engaged with these incredible women of God, I began to grow and change in ways I couldn't have imagined before. The fact that you are holding this book in your hands kinda proves Jim Rohn's point. Hanging out with the Redbuds improved my average.

Take a moment to think about where you are in your life. What are your spiritual, vocational (this includes mothering), educational, or emotional goals? Are there women in your circles who excel in those areas? Be intentional about spending more time with them. If that isn't an option, try connecting with like-minded people or groups on social media. My Facebook friends can't run over chicken soup when I'm sick or babysit my kids in a pinch, but I love them dearly, and man, can they parse Greek! Plus, there's no one like an out-of-town friend when you need a gossip-free prayer partner.

Jim may have been overstating the matter, but the people we spend time with, both in person and online, have an incredible influence on our lives. Seek out people who can help you grow, and improve your average!

Everyday Spiritual Disciplines

By Catherine McNiel

I took my young children to a meditative prayer walk. Can you imagine? In a courtyard created to inspire silence and peace, my three kids *tried* to walk slowly and speak softly. Of course, the race and roar that resulted was anything but meditative. I gathered up my parched spirit, a few shreds of dignity, and my energetic off-spring and made a beeline for the exit. Begging forgiveness from the other prayer walkers, I was struck by what a powerful metaphor the whole fiasco was for this season of my life.

Do I want to seek after God? Yes! But one thing after another in this season of small things stands in my way. All this creating and nurturing softens my heart to the creator and nurturer of us all, and I want to ponder all these things stored up in my heart. But every moment is crowded with crisis and chaos. The second I finally arrange a moment of peace is the moment someone dumps out the flour bag or someone's diaper leaks onto the rug. No matter how hopefully I set out to feed my soul, the requirements of motherhood get in the way.

Still, I see God every day.

I see him in the sacrifice and service that motherhood requires, as I give of myself to others again and again. I see him in the creation of new life, as my children grow from cells in my body to their own unique selves. And isn't this exactly the scenario spiritual practices are designed for—taking us to the end of ourselves, where we discover the beauty and faithfulness of God?

I want to attend Bible studies and service projects and prayer walks, but we *all* know how those attempts turn out. My mantra these days is *If you can't bring the mother to the spiritual practices, bring the spiritual practices to the mother.*

What does this look like in my real life? It means that instead of attending prayer walks, I walk through grocery store aisles, down the stairs to the laundry room, and across town to the park. But as I go, I keep those meditative principles in mind—reminding myself as I take one step after another that my feet are firmly planted on the ground, firmly planted in *him*.

It means I'm not singing in the choir or worship team, but when I'm folding laundry or washing dishes I crank my favorite worship songs and sing along.

It means that I'm not fasting right now, as my children need the sustenance my body produces. But when I find myself desperately hungry for a good gift from God—whether a moment to myself or an adult conversation—I use that longing to remember that God is the one who fills the gap between what we have and what we need. I use that longing to practice contentment.

When I'm driving my kids to swimming lessons and the chaos inside and outside the car has me going batty? No spiritual guru could conceive of a better environment for practicing the discipline of patience.

My day as a mom provides precious little opportunity for the quiet reflection and meditation my soul longs for, but ample opportunity to practice deep breaths and remain present in situations that take me far beyond myself; it is a rich harvest of moments to fight through the stress and into gratitude. One step, one breath, one moment at a time.

I still try to sneak off to meditative prayer walks when I get a morning to myself, but in the meantime, I'm bringing those principles to my daily chaos. And I see him here, at the end of myself, every day.

Catherine McNiel writes to open eyes to the creative and redemptive work of God in each present moment. Her Bible studies, devotions, and essays can be found in various publications and at www.catherinemcniel.com. Catherine is the author of the forthcoming NavPress title on Motherhood as a Spiritual Discipline.

Choose a Scriptural Tagline

One of the annoying things about being a writer is that you have to develop what the publishing world calls a "brand." Like we're Beyoncé or Campbell's soup or something, instead of an unbrushed, pajama-clad mom guzzling coffee at five in the morning, trying to get a few words down before the kids wake up and it's time to shower for work (just theoretically, I mean). But they have a point. What defines you as a writer? What do people expect when they pick up your book, or click on a link with your name on it? Sometimes, writers have to come up with a clever tagline that sums up their brand: Confessions of a Wannabe World Changer, or the like.

But you know what? As much as I enjoy complaining about that phenomenon, I think every mom needs a brand. What defines you as a follower of Christ? What do people expect when they see you walking toward them at church or when they pull up your contact info on their phone? If you had to come up with one verse that sums up where you are or where you want to be in your walk with Christ, what would it be?

Enter the scriptural tagline, or what some would call a "life verse."

Personally, I don't love the term "life verse." I'd prefer something like "month verse" or "season verse" or "until-the-end-of-summer-vacation-or-the-baby-sleeps-through-the-night verse." But the idea is the same. Choose one passage of Scripture that really speaks to you, commit it to memory, and binge on it, allowing it to sink deep into your soul. Whisper it to yourself throughout the day. Use a dry erase marker to write it on your bathroom mirror. Scribble it on a Post-It and stick it in your wallet or on your computer monitor.

Incorporate it into an art project, set it to music, custom order a canvas to display it in your living room—whatever you need to do to make it stick.

A quick word about memorization. Some of you started hyperventilating when you saw that word, but this ain't Awana, and I'm a big believer in crowns, jewels, and gold stars for everyone. You don't have to memorize the entire passage perfectly. In fact, unless the passage is very short, don't bother. Read the passage over and over. Get a good sense for it. Then chose one short, pithy phrase that brings the whole passage to mind, and commit that to memory.

For instance, say your verse is Jeremiah 17:7–8: "But blessed is the one who trusts in the LORD, whose confidence is in him. They will be like a tree planted by the water that sends out its roots by the stream. It does not fear when heat comes; its leaves are always green. It has no worries in a year of drought and never fails to bear fruit." Fabulous passage, but way too long to fit on a Post-It note! You can memorize the whole thing if you want, or you can use "They will be like a tree" to ping your spiritual memory. It conjures up the beautiful imagery and deep truths of the passage, and it even rhymes!

So, what is your scriptural tagline? Maybe a passage popped right into your mind, but if not, spend some time searching the Scriptures (and Google) to find one. What issues are you struggling with? What traits are you aspiring to? What truth do you need to be reminded of, over and over again? Think it over, but don't obsess. After all, "All Scripture is God-breathed and is useful for teaching" (2 Tim. 3:16), and you can always choose another scriptural tagline later.

32

Lay Down the Perfectionism

Just in case you couldn't guess, based on the fact that I'm writing a book full of Bright Ideas and bossy-pants advice, I am an oldest child. In fact, I am the oldest child of two oldest children, and the oldest grandchild on both sides. That makes me like the Übermensch of eldest children, responsible for upholding family honor by being a complete and total Goody Two-shoes and badgering the rest of my generation to fall into line. You've heard of patriarchs and matriarchs? I am the sororarch, sister-ruler of the Williams Clan.

In other words, I can be completely neurotic.

I was blessed to be raised in a family that had high expectations. It wasn't that I was pressured to attain a certain goal; to become a concert pianist or go into medicine or law. It was more that I felt the need to be like Mary Poppins—practically perfect in every way. I am not entirely sure whether that filtered down from my parents or if I was just born that way, but in any case, I somehow acquired the (subconscious) belief that I was not only capable of being perfect, but morally obligated to be so. I experienced every failure as a moral deficiency. Got 93 percent on a test? FAIL. Shame on me for not studying harder—I don't even deserve to graduate! If I was not firing on all cylinders at any given moment, I felt as if I were letting God, my family, and everyone else around me down.

Like I said, completely neurotic.

This was survivable when I was a child, able to focus on the things I excelled at while my parents sheltered me from the rest. But then I became an adult and realized that I was not, in fact, as perfect as I wanted to be. That sometimes I was a flat-out mess. I was also hit hard by the reality that there were some things I couldn't fix or control, such as my firstborn's autism, or problems at my husband's workplace. These harsh realizations led to a crisis not so much of faith, but of relationship. How did God feel about me if I could not be perfect, or even maintain the illusion of having it all together? How did *I* feel about me? And why was it so much harder for me to be gracious with myself than I believed God was with me?

Sisters, perfectionism is poison. It sucks all the joy out of life, forcing you to perform, and responding with critique instead of encouragement. Worse, it makes us pressure others to dance to its exhausting tune, lest their sloppy performance reflect badly on us. Perfectionism is idolatry, drawing our sense of self-worth from our abilities and outcomes instead of from our identity in Christ.

If I am honest, I am not sure how to help you fight your battle against perfectionism. (Did I just admit that out loud?) Grappling with my own perfectionism and the shame I experienced when I couldn't measure up to my own standards was one of the hardest, most painful things I have ever done, and I did not go into that battle willingly. But perhaps I can encourage you if life is chipping away at your Mary Poppins gloss—if divorce, or chronic illness, or job loss, or other difficult circumstances are wreaking havoc on the perfect life and perfect family you imagined for yourself. Your worth does not come from being a good person who has it all together. Your worth does not come from your marital status, or your career, or how your kids behave, or how your house looks. Your worth comes from being created in the image of God, beloved by him.

Oh, sisters. We need to ease our grip on earthly concerns, and focus on loving God and others well, cultivating mercy, compassion, and patience that can be given as well as received.

Don't Read the Bible

Okay, okay, the title of this Bright Idea may be a bit misleading. But if you grew up in an environment that had very strong opinions about what your "quiet time" should look like (half an hour in the morning, extra points if you kept study notebooks), it may free you up to realize you don't have to do it that way. Particularly since asking sleep-deprived moms to wake up before their children to do their devotions borders on cruelty. Seriously, love—God created you to need sleep. He's not disappointed in you. He delights in you!

When my kids were tiny, I functioned best finding a quiet hour or so to really dig into the Scriptures, and then meditating on what I'd learned in my studies all week. I felt guilty that I wasn't reading every day, but then, I felt guilty about pretty much everything when I was in my twenties and juiced up on mommy hormones. Giving so much space to guilt turned out to be way more detrimental to my walk with God (and everyone else) than my nontraditional Bible study habits. Take a cue from your Elsa-obsessed daughter: let it go!

I have friends who are just the opposite of me. Reading a bit of the Bible each day, even if it's just a few verses, helps them stay on an even keel. Bible apps with reading plans are incredible for people like this (and for anyone, really), and there are so many options available. Do a Google search for Bible apps and try a couple out. I bet you'll find one you love. And let's be honest—checking your phone when you've got a few minutes feels a lot more doable than tracking down your dusty Bible, lighting a candle, and settling into your favorite chair only to be interrupted by a screaming toddler. It's like they can sense when you're taking a moment for yourself, and feel obligated to remind you that THEY HAVE NEEDS TOO. But checking your phone? Totally incognito. In fact, I know one mom who is part of a texting Bible study. The leader sends the passage out in a group text, and everyone replies with their thoughts throughout the day. It's not for this mama, but it might be a fun thing to try with your girlfriends.

Personally, my life was transformed when I downloaded an audio version of *The Message* paraphrase of the Gospels. I had read them goodness knows how many times, but there was something about *hearing* the story of Jesus and his early followers, in common language, that opened me up to the work God wanted to do in and through me in a new way. That shouldn't be surprising, as the Scriptures were written to be read out loud. They had to be, since for most of human history few people were able to read, much less own books. I still have a soft spot for audio Bibles, and often listen to them on my commute or while I'm doing household chores. My husband, who is a musician and auditory learner extraordinaire, uses audio Bibles almost exclusively for his daily devotions. You can listen for free at www.BibleGateway.com.

And let's not downplay the awesomeness of children's storybook Bibles. Sure, they're highly abridged, but the best ones include stories you may not have considered in a long time, particularly if you've spent more time in the New Testament than the Old. Remember when Jael took down Sisera with a tent peg? Remember how King David adopted Mephibosheth? Remember when that little slave girl advised her master on how to get rid of leprosy? No? Then consider investing in a good Bible storybook and reading it to your kids. Some of them are available in ebook and audiobook format as well, which makes them perfect for car rides.

There are so, so many ways to engage with the Bible. Don't stress out trying to force yourself into the mold your youth pastor said was best—experiment, see what works for you, and go with it.

Tame Your Tongue

When I was born, my Auntie Lin gave me a wall hanging inscribed with my name, its meaning, and a verse plucked from Proverbs 31: "She openeth her mouth with wisdom; and in her tongue is the law of kindness" (31:26 KJV). It was the first verse I learned by heart, the calligraphy staring out at me from the puffy calico frame morning, noon, and night. In the simple logic of a child, I thought the plaque described what people named Jenny were supposed to be—that wise and kind speech were the birthright of Jennys down throughout history. I aspired to live it, whispering the words over and over in my mind. "She openeth her mouth with wisdom; and in her tongue is the law of kindness."

I was a silly little kid who had no idea that wall hangings did not, in fact, define a person's destiny. But that didn't matter to God, who used that plaque to impress the importance of wise, kind speech on my developing brain. My Auntie Lin (who was, ironically, a fiery redhead who had no problem speaking her mind) lost her fierce battle with skin cancer over a decade ago, but I still think of the monumental gift she gave me every time I read Proverbs.

Wise speech is not something we discuss much nowadays. Our culture is addicted to outrage, and oftentimes, we're more interested in winning arguments than genuinely understanding and working for the mutual benefit of people we disagree with. This is as true in evangelism as it is in politics, as true in the Christian culture wars as it is on cable news networks. If we could only convince people that we are right—if we could only win the argument with our superior proofs and witty polemic—our adversaries would have no choice but to cede the point and join our side.

Only it doesn't work that way. At least, not usually. I've known far more people who have been argued away from the kingdom of God than argued into it, especially when Christians fight dirty.

The same principle applies when speaking with our children, spouses, family, and friends. Winning a round of verbal darts may give us a sense of superiority and control, but make no mistake: harsh, thoughtless speech is incredibly destructive, even when it bullies people into giving us our way. James 3:5b–6 says "Consider what a great forest is set on fire by a small spark. The tongue also is a fire, a world of evil among the parts of the body. It corrupts the whole body, sets the whole course of one's life on fire, and is itself set on fire by hell." Those are strong words, but many could testify that foolish words have sent parts of their lives up in flames.

Taming the tongue may be difficult, especially for those of us who like to win at all costs. But wise speech is a discipline all followers of Christ are called to. It is something we can practice until we have learned how to open our mouths with wisdom and the law of kindness is imprinted on our tongues.

Hold on to the Hymns

I'll never forget the day I realized my kids didn't know the Doxology. I had grown up singing it every week as the tithes and offerings were received, but that tradition had gone the way of the dinosaur sometime before my babies were born. I guess I had assumed children's brains came preloaded with hymns—I couldn't remember not knowing them, after all—but it turns out you have to actually teach them the songs. So the Doxology became our prayer of choice before meals. You don't sing, you don't eat!

I love modern worship. There's such heartfelt beauty in the simple lyrics, and I prefer the accompaniment of a full band to the organ and piano duo I grew up with. To me, modern worship is a form of prayer and adoration. But the hymns are an incredible heritage, passed down from a time when theology was communicated in story and song to make it accessible to those who could not read. Those songs sustained the faith of our ancestors through hardships we have a hard time fathoming: hunger, slavery, immigration, epidemics, and staggering loss. And the more time I spend with elderly people, who can't remember their loved ones' names but can't forget the hymns of their childhood, the more I have come to believe the hymns could, by the grace of God, sustain us as well. The deep truths the melodies convey have a way of embedding themselves in our spiritual DNA. There's nothing magical about the hymns, but if we forgot them, it would be a great loss indeed.

As a worship leader, I try to include at least one hymn in my set list every Sunday. Sure, we do it up with drums and guitar licks, but the people I'm charged to lead know the songs. Same deal at home. As a mother, I've taken to singing the hymns to my children as lullabies at bedtime: "Great Is Thy Faithfulness," "How Great

Thou Art," and my little Swedish heart did a backflip when my youngest requested "Children of the Heavenly Father" one evening. Could there possibly be a better song to sing a child to sleep with?

Some of my friends use old hymnals (there are plenty of them floating around) in their daily devotions. If you grew up singing the hymns, try meditating on the words without music. The time spent sitting with the lyrics will add depth and richness the next time you sing it.

I like to have Pandora play instrumental hymns while I'm beading or soaking in the tub, or when I have stolen a few moments for some other quiet activity. The melodies trigger my subconscious and keep me mindful of God's presence and his faithfulness from ages past right up to today.

Maybe the problem isn't that your kids don't know the hymns. Maybe you didn't grow up with them either. That's okay, and totally fixable! You can Google lists of the most beloved hymns, pull up the words and melodies online, and find a gazillion renditions of them on YouTube. Even if it's the modern songs that speak to your soul, taking the time to learn the first verse and chorus of some of the classics, and teaching them to your children, is an investment you won't regret.

World without end! Amen, amen.

Because They Said So!

Bright Ideas from Mentor Moms

Your relationship with the Lord is the most important gift you can give your children. As my children grew from toddlers to elementary school to high school and now into college, I recognize that things went so much better when I clung to the Lord rather than to them. In whatever ways are best for you, nurture your relationship with the one who loves your children even more than you do. The gift of mom's soul care is never to be overlooked.
—Sharon R. Hoover, mama of two

Spiritual development is hard because it's hard, not because you're doing it wrong. Also, changing diapers and waking up at night totally counts as time with God. "Praise the LORD, all you servants of the LORD who minister by night in the house of the LORD." (Ps. 134:1)
—Heather Caliri, mama of two

God promises rest and calls us to rest throughout Scripture. Just as we care for the physical needs of our infants and children, watching their sleep schedules and bedtimes, we need to give ourselves the rest we need. Self-care is not selfish. Instead, by practicing rest, we receive the love and care of God into our bodies and souls.
—Leah Everson, mama of two

Practice self-forgiveness, knowing that you are imitating Christ, who practices it toward you.
—Heather Walker Peterson, mama of two

As a single mom who is trying to support my four-year-old and myself while working from home, I've learned the quality of my relationship with God can't be measured by the quantity of "alone/quiet time" I spend with God.

Instead, I find my most precious connections with God in the moments with my son, in pausing for a thirty-second prayer when tempers are flaring, and accepting there is no one way to do this messy adventure of mothering.
—Natalie Nyquist, mama of one

Discover new ways to connect with God if the old ways (such as morning prayer and Scripture) seem impossible. Take a stroller walk in a forest, enjoy the perfect latte near a stream, or watch a soul-stirring movie.
—Beth Bruno, mama of three

During the busy years with my seven young ones it was challenging to fit in my own quality devotional time, until I allowed God to minister to my heart while daily reading Bible stories from the children's Bible to my kids. Those simple truths refreshed me as my children cuddled close to hear God's Word.
—PeggySue Wells, mama of seven

I don't journal every day, nor do I use it like a diary. Instead, I write out my prayers and fears, or my joys. I'm amazed glancing through these journals I've written for years now: I see all the Ebenezers God's left in my path that I'd forgotten. Journals help me remember God is always at work, especially when I can't stop to notice it.
—Erin F. Wasinger, mama of three

Pay attention to the tenderness with which you love your kid, and then remember that that's just the teeniest glimpse of the tenderness with which God loves you.
—Bronwyn Lea, mama of three

Notes

[1] Ken Block, "Change Your Mind," © 2000 by Universal.

[2] Jonathan Oatman Jr., "Count Your Blessings," in *Songs for Young People* by Edwin Excell, (Cincinnati: Curts and Jennings, 1897).

[3] Ibid.

POWER OUTLET TWO

Loving Your Neighbor . . . Like, Your Actual Neighbor

I love my neighbors, but there's a reason we all live in the country. The people to the west have hunting dogs that bay and bawl at all hours of the night. The neighbors to the north have chickens, which wouldn't be so bad except for this one neurotic rooster. On the south side of our property, my brother lives in a 1960s mobile home perched on cement blocks. And my neighbors to the east like to rip the doors off our garbage shed and snack on our trash (bears are known to do that).

Of course, if you ask my neighbors, they could tell you all about my boys' loud "disagreements," the broken toys scattered all over the lawn, and my husband's teenaged music students skidding down the hill on bald tires.

I'm sure my neighbors have several complaints. Well, except for the bears. They're cool with whatever, as long as we keep the gravy train rollin'.

It's easy to talk about loving our neighbors when we're envisioning some poor, deserving mother in a land far away. It's harder when our neighbor is an actual person with noisy kids and obnoxious dogs, who love to drag your trash out into the open for all to see. We get excited about feeding programs in Guatemala but prefer to ignore that the mouthy kid down the cul-de-sac is dangerously overweight because he subsists on Doritos and Ho Hos while his mom is working her third job.

See, the closer we are to people, the easier it is to judge them. We see their flaws, and they see ours. But it's judgment that keeps us from loving our neighbor well. We build walls to distance ourselves from people we have judged unworthy of our time and attention, and to protect ourselves from people who we fear are judging us. It's like middle school all over again. Maybe we're not shoving people into lockers, but we're also not buddying up with the chain-smoking bottle-blonde who cycles through men like dirty laundry. And we snark about what a self-righteous snob the PTA president is because women like her make us feel insecure. We're bulletproof, baby, but we don't dare step outside our own little Popemobiles to engage in the risk of authentic relationship.

But Jesus came to tear down those walls. To reconcile us not just to God, but to one another.

In this section, we're going to be talking about some of the ways that we can love our neighbors. Like, our *actual* neighbors. Are you ready? Take a deep breath, unfasten your seat belt, and prepare to exit the Popemobile.

Park in Play Areas

When my kids were tiny, I spent an inordinate amount of time at McDonald's PlayPlace. Yeah, I know, the food is nasty (in more ways than one), and the play equipment should require hazmat suits, but you've got to understand: I live in Northern Wisconsin, where we have about three days of nice weather per year. My husband worked at a church half an hour from our home, and we only had one car. I had to drop him off early on Sunday mornings and figure out something to do with the kids for two hours until Sunday school started. There was no way I was going to chase them around the church, but driving home seemed like a waste of time and gas. Besides, if I went home, the kids would just strip naked the moment they walked through the door, and all that work getting them ready would be lost.

Enter McDonald's PlayPlace.

It's safe to say that most adults hanging out in a fast-food play area aren't there for the ambiance. These are desperate people, drawn into the vortex of hard plastic booths and hard plastic burgers at the behest of hangry (hungry + angry) children who are on their parents' last nerve. But the more time I spent in play areas, the more I realized that these weren't all shiny, happy families in the first place. There were a lot of kids being handed off from one parent's custody to another or playing under the watchful eye of a tired-looking social worker. There were single moms trying to get their schoolwork done, and kids with special needs struggling to interact with their peers, and families taking a much-needed break from hospital vigils.

It's amazing what you see in fast-food joints once you start paying attention. Cheap fries are a great equalizer. If Jesus were walking the earth today, I bet he'd hang out at Mickey D's instead of some snooty coffee shop. I mean, think about it.

I have had many holy experiences and God-ordained conversations in the unlikely sanctuary of the Golden Arches. And even when the atmosphere was more "battle of Armageddon" than "blessed communion," every bratty, screaming kid (sometimes they were mine) and exhausted, cranky adult (sometimes it was me) provided an opportunity to practice the fine art of loving my neighbor, of extending grace and the occasional strawberry milkshake.

Next time your kids get hangry and you succumb to the siren song of cheap burgers and—let's admit it—really addictive fries, pray that God will make you attentive to the people around you. Instead of hiding behind your Kindle, start a conversation with someone who looks open. Offer up a silent prayer for the little boy who can't seem to interact appropriately. Flash an understanding smile at the mom who looks about to crack, and tell her you'll keep her kids from running out into the street while she takes her toddler to the bathroom.

Just don't forget to douse your kids in hand sanitizer before loading them back into the van.

Go Clubbing

For several years, I spent one night per month at a hipster café an hour from my home, eating sweet potato fries and arguing about the proper use of semicolons with a group of people drawn together by our shared love of speculative fiction. It was about the strangest mash-up of people you could imagine: Linda, who wrote sweeping fantasy epics while counting down the days to retirement; Jim, a sci-fi enthusiast who had majored in Russian at Macalester back in the seventies, for reasons he couldn't explain even to himself; Lacey, a young Catholic progressive who wrote scathing commentaries on the church's sexual ethics; Marie, a middle-aged marine biologist with a thing for werewolves; and me, the Jesus-girl always trying to force awkward spiritual analogies onto the texts. But we were a family. And we had a good laugh every time a new server handed Jim the bill, assuming he was the patriarch of our weird little familia.

These are not people I would have met if I hadn't joined that writing group. And my life would have been so much poorer for it.

When our kids are young, it's really easy to live our lives inside a Christian bubble, especially if we are stay-at-home moms. Breaking free and developing meaningful relationships with people outside the church requires some thought and intentionality. One of the most surefire ways of doing this is to join some sort of secular club, group, or society.

Just to be clear, I'm not suggesting that you join a club for the express purpose of evangelizing the members. That's obnoxious, and they'll smell your intentions a mile off. But we are not meant to live in a Christian ghetto, and let's be honest: some of us get weird if we don't spend enough time with people who aren't believers. It's like those moms who don't get out enough, and wind up cutting their friend's steak into bite-sized pieces and using words like "wee-wee" when they finally have a girls' night out. Yes, we've all done it, but do not go gently into that good night! A similar thing happens when we only hang out with Christians. Before we know it, we're tagging everything #blessed, participating in the latest vaguely Christian home-based-business scheme, and girl-crushing on that Hillsong United chick. Just don't go there, friends. Just don't go there.

Hop on Google, nab a local alternative paper, check out Meetup .com, or head down to the library to find out what clubs, associations, and special interest groups meet in your area. Bust out of your bubble and develop real, meaningful relationships with people outside the faith, blessing them and allowing them to bless you. And bonus—you get to engage in something you really love.

Here's to making new friends, and not being (too) weird.

Loving the Blight of the Neighborhood

By Marlena Graves

I sit on my couch and look out my window and across Main Street. We are new to our town, but I have tried to learn a little bit about my neighbors.

The neighbors across Main Street and to our left are grandparents. The grandfather is either mentally ill or suffering from dementia; it's hard to tell which. In the summer, if we're outside and they have their windows open, we can sometimes hear the grandma hollering at the two grandkids. The grandkids, a young boy and young girl, are elementary school–aged and seem to have a rough life with absentee parents. They roam the neighborhood unsupervised. Once, they turned our spigot on so they could fill their water guns, which we wouldn't have minded if we had been home to ask, and if they hadn't forgotten to turn the faucet off all the way. The only reason we found out about their illicit use of our spigot was because our next-door neighbor told us her husband shooed them away.

Around 11 P.M. a few weeks ago, I heard sirens and saw the flashing lights of several cop cars, a fire truck, and an ambulance. The emergency vehicles parked on Main Street directly in front of their house. I was worried the grandfather had experienced some sort of heart attack or mental breakdown. I opened our door and stepped onto the porch. I said a prayer and stepped back inside without figuring out what had happened. The next-day, I found out the little girl's father (or maybe it's her mother's current boyfriend) was arrested for drug possession.

Several of the neighbors around here consider that family to be the blight on this otherwise good neighborhood. A nuisance. But I try hard to see them the way Jesus sees them. I have compassion on them because I remember what it was like to be poor. I sometimes wonder if my family of origin was considered the blight of our neighborhood because of our poverty.

Every now and then, the grandfather will drop the grandkids off at our house so they can play with our daughters. I invite the kids to VBS. They decline. I worry that they believe they're not good enough, or worthy enough, to go with us, though we've done the best we can to welcome them to our home while maintaining healthy boundaries and proper supervision.

It would be easy to distance ourselves, or our children, from this struggling family. Some would probably applaud that decision. But Jesus tells us to love our neighbors, and these kids and their grandparents are our neighbors. Besides, I have a solid hunch that Jesus would visit their house first if he were taking a tour of our neighborhood.

Marlena Graves (MDiv) is the author of A Beautiful Disaster: Finding Hope in the Midst of Brokenness *(Brazos Press 2014). Hearts & Minds bookstore awarded it the Best Book on Spiritual Formation by a First Time Writer (2014). Marlena is also a bylined writer for* Christianity Today, Our Daily Journey (Our Daily Bread), *and other venues, and is on staff at her church.*

Throw a Party

My friend Shannon is one of the most intentional mamas I know. A whip-smart marketer with a quick smile and an earnest faith, she is perpetually reaching out to people who don't know Jesus, and thinking up ways to help people grow in their faith. I am not sure if she even realizes she is doing it, but you can't brush past that woman without being discipled in some way. She is a gift to the body of Christ and beyond.

I could probably write a whole book of Shannon stories, but I am going to share one of my favorites, because it is so fun and pull-off-able. Several years back, a retired teacher from our church (she had actually been my first grade teacher) moved to South Africa to serve as a house mother in an orphanage for medically fragile children. Most of the children she cared for were HIV positive and not eligible for adoption, but one little boy was suffering from hydrocephalus. He had been receiving medical attention, but he desperately needed a level of treatment the home just couldn't afford.

When Shannon heard about this, she snapped into action. Now, people up where I live throw a lot of benefits, usually involving copious amounts of spaghetti served up in town halls that haven't been renovated since the 1960s. But not Shannon. No, Shannon and her family were going to throw a party to raise the money for the little boy's medical expenses, complete with games, a pig roast, and a cotton candy machine. They basically turned their yard into party central and invited the entire church, of nearly seven hundred people, over to play. Talk about transforming the neighborhood!

Needless to say, the little boy got the care he needed. Shannon gets stuff done.

Here's the thing that strikes me about this. What Shannon and her family did was not all that complicated. It took time and effort, yes, but what it really took was resolve and follow-through. The vast majority of us are capable of throwing a party. We probably do it several times a year. What we struggle with is moving from idea to action.

So let's practice, shall we? Why not take a page from Shannon's book and throw a party to benefit a cause you care about? It could be a big to-do that takes up the entire block, or a simple gathering in your living room. You could throw your fête in a banquet room, or your church basement, or a roller rink, or at the beach. Maybe you could just throw the same old parties you always have, but ask the attendees to bring donations for the local food pantry or make a contribution to a certain cause instead of bringing gifts.

Everyone loves a celebration, and knowing that it's benefiting a good cause just adds to the joy. Let's move from idea to action and get the party started!

Stop Slamming Immigrants

"I think there was a little Mexican boy following you around." I stared at the pretty blonde woman, stunned. I was trying to pay for the stroller I had found at her garage sale, but couldn't find the twenty-dollar bill I had stashed in my pocket. Her theory about how it had gone missing was different than mine, to say the least. Had I been 33 instead of 23, more secure in my ability to speak up with grace and confidence, I would have called her out on it. As it was, I just got in my car and drove off, sans stroller.

I found the bill wadded up in another pocket later.

The woman's words had shocked me, not because I didn't know racism was a significant problem in farm towns flooded with migrant workers, but because she was so up front about it. Apparently, she thought that was a perfectly acceptable thing to say to another white woman. The older I get, however, the less shocked I become. Hearing people say nasty, suspicious, dehumanizing things about immigrants has become almost passé.

But this sort of garbage rhetoric has absolutely no place among followers of Christ.

I know that immigration is a controversial political topic, and I understand why. Government exists to keep order, and no matter how much I'd love to fling the doors open and invite everyone in, just as God has done for us, we are not God, nor does any one nation have God's unlimited resources at their complete disposal. But no matter what your stance is on immigration policy, the Bible has only one witness on how we are to treat the immigrants who do come: "For the LORD your God is God of gods and Lord of lords, the great God, mighty and awesome, who shows no partiality and accepts no bribes. He defends the cause of the fatherless and the widow, and loves the foreigner residing among you, giving them food and clothing. And you are to love those who are foreigners, for you yourselves were foreigners in Egypt." (Deut. 10:17–19)

We are called to love, not disdain. To speak life, not slander. To remember that immigrants are fellow human beings created in the image of God, and that to view them or speak of them as anything less than sacred and inestimably precious is an insult to our common creator.

And let's remember this: Jesus was an immigrant too.

There is no shortage of news anchors, pundits, and politicians who make a living fanning the flames of outrage against people God loves. And I can understand why some people are angry. But oh, friends . . . in your anger, do not sin.

Invite People into Your Messy Life

By Bronwyn Lea

Some say that they love Pinterest because they find it inspirational. I disagree. The word that comes to mind for me is "terrifying." I have been known to introduce myself this way: "Hi, I'm Bronwyn, and I'm a walking Pinterest-fail."

It's true. I am.

And for the longest time, I was afraid that my inability to keep things neat, much less make them beautiful, meant I would never be good at hospitality.

But more and more I'm realizing that Inigo Montoya was right: "You keep using that word. I don't think it means what you think it means" *(Princess Bride)*.

If motherhood has taught me anything, it is that hospitality is not about perfect place settings and artful Instagrammable lunches. Hospitality is about the warmth of our welcome. It is less about how much space we have in our homes. It is about how much space we have in our hearts.

In fact, in nearly a dozen Slavic languages, the word for hospitality literally means "bread and salt." Hospitality is not limited to those occasions when we display our finest, but means welcoming others into sharing life's basics with us. It's more sandwich than soufflé, more fast mac and cheese than filet mignon.

Hospitality means welcoming people, even if it's simple, incomplete, and messy. It was a lesson I learned the first time I visited my new friend, Jana. "Oh, sorry about the laundry," she said, sweeping bras and underwear to the side of the couch to make space for

57

me to sit. "It's okay," I laughed. "Now I feel safe sharing my dirty laundry with you too."

For it's true: there's something about letting people see the jumbled mess of our space that lets them know that you can cope with jumbled messes. And who of us is not a bit of a jumbled mess, in need of a safe place to be ourselves?

In the years since I found that warm, welcome spot on Jana's messy couch, I have found myself all the more ready to invite others into our mess. "Come on over, but be warned . . . I won't clean before you come. You are welcome into our real life, where we make *real mess*." Real mess. Real joy. Real life.

Come on in. Kick off your shoes. Help yourself to a sandwich, and watch out for the sticky patch on the floor. Your jumbled self is most welcome here. Mi casa, su casa.

Bronwyn Lea is a South African–born writer, speaker, and mom to three little ones. She writes about the holy messes in family, faith, and culture at www.bronlea.com and various other places around the web. She and her husband live in California, where she perseveres in her search for the perfect homemade ice-cream recipe.

Go Outside

AS I write this, I am sitting on a park bench overlooking the rocky shore of Lake Superior, trying to avoid getting bombed by seagulls. The boardwalk is milling with a kaleidoscope of happy, open people—Muslims to Mennonites, local kids to vacationing seniors—enjoying the perfect Duluth day. My laptop and I are not being particularly good neighbors, but hey, at least we're out here. Anything could happen.

It's nothing short of astonishing how little time people spend outdoors nowadays. We country folk may be more aware of it than most, and compensate with gardening and vitamin D supplements, but many of my suburban friends are running a devastating deficit. When I visited my parents a year after they moved into a new housing development, they confessed that they had only met one of their neighbors. The only people they ever saw outside were serious-looking joggers, sunglasses fixed on the horizon and earbuds firmly in place.

Attached garages may seriously be the downfall of American society.

This is one aspect of being a good neighbor where moms have a clear advantage. Sure, taking our munchkins out in public can be a dubious prospect. Some outings are bound to end in disaster. But there are few groupings of human beings more relatable than a mother with young children who don't have social filters. Bonus points if you have a friendly, fluffy dog. Getting your kids out into the sunshine and fresh air is not only good for them (and you), it's a great way to interact with real, live human beings.

Make a point of taking your kids to public areas where they can meet new playmates, and you can connect with the people in your neighborhood. Parks, beaches, summer concert series, and local walk-up ice-cream shops are great places to strike up conversations and initiate relationships with new and interesting people. If you're the shy sort, don't worry—there are probably many people who would love to have a conversation with you, if you don't look petrified. Ditch the sunglasses, stow your phone, and grin at the mom whose kid just flung sand in your toddler's eyes (you might want to be more circumspect if it was your kid doing the flinging, but apologies make good icebreakers too). They say the strongest bonds are formed in adversity, and if parenting in public doesn't qualify, I don't know what does.

When my kids were little, I kept a tote bag of supplies in the trunk to make impromptu trips to the beach, or the park, or the zoo more doable. Sunblock, granola bars, a change of clothes, and an extra box of wipes—keeping them in the car meant I could take people up on last-minute invitations or give into my children's pleas to do something fun without having to trek home. I also had the opportunity to share the occasional towel, or snack, or dry pair of pants with parents who found themselves in a tight spot. It's amazing how life-giving the words "I have an extra diaper" can be.

A little preparation can go a long way in making it easy (well, comparatively easy) to take your kids outside. It's good for them, it's good for you, and it's a great way to meet your neighbors.

Smile

Smile.

That's it. Just smile. Look people in the eye, acknowledging that they are actual human beings worthy of your regard, and smile.

Okay, disclaimer time. I know this suggestion makes some people cringe. Many of us have contended with smarmy men demanding smiles as we pass them on the street, or older women insisting that we bury our unreliable emotions, paint a pleasing quirk onto our lips, and fake it until we make it. That's not what I'm talking about. Others have faces that naturally look very serious when they're relaxed, and they're sick to death of being pestered about it. That's not what I'm talking about either.

I also understand that smiling is not always a good idea. I travel to Chicago pretty regularly and will be the first to admit that the expression I wear while riding the CTA public transit bears little resemblance to the one I wear while browsing the Hardware Hank in Poplar, Wisconsin. It takes a lot of work for this country girl to look so world-weary and disinterested, and I rely heavily on my movie-star sunglasses, but I do it. But even in Chicago, there are people to smile at. Cab drivers and grocers and people walking dogs and, yes, even the occasional person on the CTA.

The world would be a nicer place if people just smiled more.

Smiling is good for you. It lowers stress, releases endorphins, and even boosts your immune system. It's easier than exercise! And when you smile at people, they usually smile back, reaping the same benefits you just enjoyed.

Smiling also makes you seem more approachable. I understand that this is why some people avoid smiling in public, but friends, that exasperated mom wrangling three squirmy children or that stooped old man trying to pick up the newspaper he dropped are probably not out to get you. Be wise, yes, but don't be paranoid. If we want to change the world, we have to be willing to interact with it from time to time.

If the idea of smiling at strangers makes you anxious, practice on the greeters at Walmart. That's basically their job—to smile at people. And unless they're having a really bad day, if you shoot a dazzling smile right back at them, those sweet little pensioners will usually grin like they've just won the lottery. People love being looked at like human beings who actually matter, especially if they're usually ignored.

Smile. Just smile. It will do you and the world a world of good.

Invite People Home for the Holidays

Christmas Eve has always been my favorite day of the year. In the evening, before the church service, my father's extended family all crams into someone's house to exchange gifts and gorge on Christmas cookies, Chex Mix, and grandma's homemade buns, slathered with this weird hot dog and pickle spread. It's a complete free-for-all—close to forty large, laughing people talking all over each other, while toddlers zip under their legs and children run circles through the living room. I'm sure that sounds horrible to some people, but I adore my big, crazy family and can't imagine anything better.

Not everyone has a big, crazy family, though, and even if they do, they may not be able to visit them for the holidays. That's why you should invite them to celebrate with your big, crazy family! Hey, your house is already as spiffy as it gets, and you're making a boatload of food anyway. Why not invite that older couple who just moved into the area, or that single friend from work, or the divorcé who lives next door and is spending his first Christmas without his kids?

Stand-in family has always been a vital part of my life. The most difficult thing about the years my family spent in Liberia was being separated from our extended family. But Uncle Richard and Mohammed were constant figures in our home, and Uncle Johnny made it official by marrying my aunt. An older couple on the mission base agreed to be "Grandma and Grandpa Lueders" (I still have a little wire doll they gave me), and while people came and went, there was always at least one missionary family who felt more like kinfolk than friends. We spent Christmases, Easters, Thanksgivings, and birthdays with these people, and while it didn't erase the ache of missing my real family, it did ease it. I haven't seen some of them since we left Liberia in 1988, but they are still precious to me. My childhood would have been impoverished without them, and they may as well be blood.

Perhaps you can be that special person to someone in your community, or find someone who will become that to you and your children. Have the courage to reach out, and invite people home for the holidays. You may find that other people are as hungry for connection—and pumpkin pie—as you are.

Because They Said So!

Bright Ideas from Mentor Moms

It may seem kind of simple, but in today's world, when people connect online as much as in person sometimes, think about opening up your social media world to neighbors. We had lived next to a family for three years and talked in passing. When I "friended" them on Facebook, I discovered they were raising money for an adoption. We were able to help out, and it opened up a whole new relationship. We were able to watch their pets and take them to the airport when they flew out for the adoption. All because we reached out and found out a bit more about them.
—Nicole T. Walters, mama of two

For a few weeks in a row, do your laundry at the local laundry mat, even if you don't need to. Ask total strangers how to work the change machine or the super-size washer. You'll strike up some interesting conversations and probably help a person or two.
—Margaret Philbrick, mama of three

About once a year, I invite all the women in my neighborhood over for tea, in their PJs, and I promise not to clean my house. Then, I ask them to invite all the women they know in the neighborhood as well. I end up with a group of women I would never have otherwise known, and it is a huge blessing for all of us.
—Catherine McNiel, mama of three

Help your children brainstorm nice things they could do for the neighbors. Maybe they could draw a picture for the woman across the street, or rake a neighbor's leaves, or give the girl at the end of the block that Barbie dress she really likes. Teach your children to pay attention to the people around them and be on the lookout for ways to serve.
—Jenny Rae Armstrong, mama of four

Never pass up a child's lemonade stand! I've met several of our neighbors through their children's entrepreneurial efforts. A parent often emerges from the house while I'm enjoying the tasty treat, and we can chat. One time, a lemonade stand offered only ice water, but the precious little guy with his enormous, proud grin made me quite happy to pay for my "lemonade."
—Sharon R. Hoover, mama of two

Be intentional. Take the time to talk and listen. Garden often in your front yard. Walk your dog at the same time every morning. That led me to a delightful every-morning walk with my neighbor for the past five or six years.
—Afton Rorvik, mama of two

At least once every summer, invite your block to a barbecue at your place. Stick funny invites in their mailbox with an RSVP number. They will gladly call you back, and most will show up. Even if they don't RSVP or show up, they will wave to you as you drive down the street, for months. Invites equal gratitude.
—Margaret Philbrick, mama of three

It's easy to love your neighbor with food. Begin there. When we lived next to a couple in their eighties, we shared meals (they don't mind kids' poor manners), half pots of soup when they were ill, and rolls and bread passed over the fence. We spoke love with leftover containers and warm carbs wrapped in wax paper long before we said it aloud.
—Erin F. Wasinger, mama of three

POWER OUTLET THREE

Keep the Change: Shopping for a Better World

My friend Esther Emery lives in a yurt. No, she's not a missionary to Mongolia; she's a homestead wife and mama of three from Idaho. I was Skyping with her the other day (yes, her yurt has Internet) about the whys and hows of her off-grid lifestyle, and she said something incredibly profound: "What makes me both radical and empowered is how I think about economics."

I'm sorry, I just have to stop here for a minute. Don't you love a woman with the chutzpah to refer to herself as "radical and empowered?" Hardcore.

But Esther is right. Whether we are consciously aware of it or not, economics colors almost every aspect of our existence. And the more money we have and the more tangled up our lives become with material goods, the more true that statement is.

The Bible contains many, many warnings about the love of money and the lure of economic advancement. It's easy for us to ignore the New Testament's warnings to the rich, because when the kids are little and we're bogged down by daycare costs and student loan repayments, many of us feel like we're barely keeping our head above water. But on a global scale, even the poorest Americans are filthy stinkin' rich. Did you know that according to the World Bank, almost half of the world lives on less than $2.50 per day? Did you know that the vast majority of people live on less than $10 per day? Did you know that if American women stopped buying cosmetics, the money they saved could cover the cost of educating every single child in the entire world?[1]

I never liked eyeliner anyway.

It's not that having money is bad. The Bible also tells many stories about people who stewarded their wealth well, using it to care for people in their communities and beyond. Jesus' own ministry was largely financed by wealthy women who traveled with him and those other twelve guys. So it can be done! But managing our resources wisely and devoting them to kingdom purposes doesn't necessarily come naturally, especially in a society where our worth is measured by the stuff we own, financial security is synonymous with responsibility, and downsizing is downright countercultural.

In the United States, 85 percent of all spending decisions are made by women.[2] We have enormous economic clout, whether we realize it or not. This next section will give you some ideas on what to do with all that influence.

We don't all have to move into yurts, but let's be radical and empowered and change the way we think about economics.

Swap before You Shop

Okay, I'll confess. As shallow and materialistic as it is, there are few things that lift my spirits more than throwing on a cute new top, or finding the perfect work tote, or trying on a pair of jeans that makes me feel like a million bucks. But getting something new doesn't necessarily require spending a lot of money. In fact, shopping in your friends' closets can be a lot more fun.

One of the churches my husband used to work at organized an annual clothing swap for gently used clothes and accessories. Everyone cleaned out their closets in the weeks leading up to the event. The night before the big swap, everything was sorted and displayed according to size. Anyone and everyone was invited to shop the swap, and the stuff that didn't get picked up was donated to the free store at a local shelter.

I got a couple cute outfits out of the deal, but the real win was in the children's section. Kids have this habit of outgrowing their clothing, no matter how high-quality, on-trend, or expensive it is. And the fact that many parents and grandparents enjoy buying high-quality, on-trend, expensive clothing for their little beanstalks definitely works to the advantage of those of us who find Target a little rich for our blood. My babies never looked so good.

Could you and your friends organize a swap at your church, maybe right before school starts, when everyone is trying to outfit their kids? In my experience, most churches are willing to host such an event, if they know someone is going to take responsibility for getting rid of the leftover clothing.

If the idea of spending a day immersed in a hundred people's cast-off clothing sounds overwhelming, never fear. Swaps work on a smaller scale as well. Recently, my friend Heather invited me to a cozy girls' night at her place, including snacks, drinks, and clothing that was still super adorable, even though their owners were sick of them. I'll admit that it's somewhat off-putting to realize how much better that hip-skimming sweater looks on your friend than it ever did on you, but hey—those cute boots you had always admired make a pretty good consolation prize. Plus, it's kind of cool to see your favorite girls strutting your stuff. People who share coffee dates are friends. People who share clothes are family.

This same principle can be applied to books, movies, and video games. I know, I know—most of my media lives on the cloud now too. But I still have shelves loaded down with once-was-enough books and DVDs, and chances are you do as well. Organize a swap before donating the rest to the public library book sale or a local retirement home. Make sure the senior citizens in your community are in on book and media swaps too. Many of them have more time than money and aren't able to access all the free stuff online. Your dog-eared Janette Oke books could make some sweet old lady's day.

It's always fun to get new things. But try to swap before you shop, and save your money for things that really matter.

Sell Your House

Okay, ladies. Are you ready for this? Take a deep breath, and make sure you are sitting down.

You should consider selling your house.

Yes, you heard me right. This idea might sound outrageous, and it's certainly not for everyone, but think about it for a minute.

Is your mortgage sucking your bank account dry, locking you into a job you don't love and demanding time and resources that could be used elsewhere? Is your free time gobbled up cleaning, maintaining, and repairing a house and yard that is far bigger than it needs to be? Could you have a greater impact if you lived in a more modest home, perhaps in a neighborhood that could use a little light?

What I'm asking is, Do you own your house, or does your house own you?

Maybe this suggestion isn't as crazy as it sounds, huh?

But do you know what is crazy? In the United States, the average house size has more than doubled since the 1950s. So while your grandma and her five siblings were raised quite comfortably in a house that was just under one thousand square feet, you and your baby brother were probably squabbling over two thousand, and you're stuck maintaining around twenty-four-hundred square feet.[3]

I mean, I get it. It's nice to have space to spread out, and the living room is the last place I want to be when one kid is on the computer, two are arguing over what to watch on TV, and the last one is throwing bouncy balls at everyone's heads. Once upon a time, such behavior would have resulted in the children being sent outside to play (gasp!). But honestly, I usually wind up beating a hasty retreat to my home office or some other quiet spot. I will be the first to admit that this pattern isn't good for our family life or, frankly, for my children's health. Kids need space to run, but building them a twenty-three-hundred square foot technological playground probably isn't the answer.

Downsizing could actually be the best thing you could do for your family.

If you're already living in a sweet little starter home, consider staying put. Just because you could upgrade doesn't mean you're required to. If you're lucky enough to have equity in your home, imagine what you could do with the proceeds if you downsized. Could you fund five wells in African villages, afford an international adoption, or create an endowment for your favorite ministry? Could you change careers, pay off your mother's house, or take your kids on a trip that would expand their cultural horizons?

Look, I'm not telling you that you need to sell your house. But just in case you never considered it, I am giving you permission to ponder the possibilities. If your home is truly your greatest material asset, how can you make it count for the kingdom?

Make a Weekly Budget

I don't know who invented those suggested budget sheets you find in financial resources, but I'm pretty sure it was someone who likes numbers more than I do. I mean, I'm a reasonably intelligent woman. But if you were to hack into the computer systems of the schools I attended and peek at my grades, you could see why I spent many years convinced that algebra existed for the sole purpose of pulling down my GPA.

That never stopped me from being fascinated by budgeting, though, especially when I was little. I remember watching my father diligently track our monthly expenses on this cool graph paper with blue and red lines. I thought it was very grown-up and impressive. But when I reached adulthood (and this was before the days of online banking, kids), every ledger book I bought turned into a diary, or a shopping list, or a sketchbook for my kids within a week. That whole number-tracking thing? Not happening.

But even though traditional budgeting was not my forte, my husband and I still needed to find a way to live within our means. We had heard of the envelope system and liked the idea of using cash for our purchases, but carrying around a bunch of envelopes containing about twenty-five dollars each seemed like overkill. And seriously, how does anyone keep their kids in shoes, backpacks, and winter coats on a budget like that? So we developed our own system.

We looked at our fixed expenses and realized that after paying our mortgage and utilities and keeping enough gas in our car to get us from here to there, we had about $600 left. We divided that by 4.5 (approximate weeks per month), and figured we had $133 to cover each week's expenses—groceries, clothing, entertainment, and whatever else. (It's a good thing we were young and in love and knew a lot of ways to spruce up mac and cheese.) We decided to carry around $120 in cash for our purchases each week, and dutifully put the extra $13.33 aside so that we could still eat when our license renewal fees came due.

Believe it or not, it worked. We not only managed to squeak by on $120 per week, but actually saved a little money.

If you're a money maven who rocks her monthly budget, that's great! Hats off to you. But if the idea of breaking down your monthly purchases makes your skin crawl, consider budgeting by the week. That way, you can keep a reign on your spending without wrestling through the numbers. And keeping our spending under control is a crucial part of stewarding our resources—not only for our own benefit, but for the good of the world and the glory of God.

Track Every Purchase

Okay, I know the last Bright Idea was all about how *not* to track your purchases. But if you want to step up your kingdom-minded money management a little, or a lot, you're going to have to get radical. Enter off-grid homestead wife and mom Esther Emery.

When I asked her to lay out some baby steps toward sustainable living for people who don't want to go off the grid, she said, "My first recommendation is that people track their purchases. It seems overly simplified to just notice how much money you're spending and what you're spending it on . . . but there's an awareness that gives you the power to make decisions."

Couldn't she have just said something about eating organic?

But Esther is right. Spending is one of those places where the Douglas County High School Class of '95 motto actually holds true: Knowledge Is Power. (I still want to know which kid thought that would be a cool motto. I mean, we had Kurt Cobain and the whole grunge movement, and that's the best we could come up with? On second thought, never mind. "Knowledge Is Power" is fine.)

Anyhow, Esther suggests that you "write down every single expenditure over a period of time, and then just follow [your heart.] Because you'll notice what drives you crazy. You'll notice what's embarrassing. You'll notice what's downright shameful."

Which is exactly why some of us *don't* track our expenses, right?

But again, Esther is right. It's so easy for money to slip through our fingers without us really realizing where it's going. Dinner out after church, seven dollars' worth of snacks at the gas station, that jacket we'll never wear from that sale we couldn't pass up, the Pampered Chef purchase we made just to be a good friend—it all adds up.

My big pointless expenditure is lunch out. Several times a week. Not an expensive lunch, mind you; we're talking five to ten bucks for a burger at Hardees, or the special at my favorite Vietnamese place, or the hot turkey sandwich at the neighborhood diner. That's fine if I really *want* to eat out, or I'm meeting a friend or something. But when I'm spending five to ten bucks a day because I didn't think ahead enough to pack a lunch before leaving for work? That money would be better spent elsewhere.

Try tracking your purchases for a month. Sure, it's a bit of a hassle, but it's not that bad if you scribble things down in real time. Even I used to do it all the time, before the advent of online banking. Then thoughtfully, prayerfully, look through your ledger book or whatever app you use to keep track. What's good about your spending habits? What's bad? What needs some trimming, tweaking, or fattening up? Then, as Esther says, follow your heart and take action.

Eat Less Meat

Back in the late 1990s, when I was a new mom, I could buy a pound of hamburger for about ninety-nine cents. Ninety-nine cents! Can you imagine? Needless to say, it didn't stay that way. I remember standing in the produce section of the grocery store during the recession of 2008, realizing that I would need to choose between meat and fruit. The fruit won.

Luckily, I already knew how to stretch a little bit of meat a long way. Pot roasts were replaced with savory stews. I quit serving chicken breasts and shredded them into Tex-Mex instead. My kids became acquainted with an insane variety of rice and beans: Cajun, Latin American, chickpea curries, and legume stews. We started making chili with turkey instead of beef. Our budget got fatter, our hearts got healthier, and the kids adapted, as kids do.

Americans eat a lot of meat, more than almost any other nation on the earth. According to the Food and Agriculture Organization of the United Nations, the average American consumes over 270 pounds of meat per year. That's pretty extreme, compared to my relatives in Norway who pack away about 150 pounds, or my friends across the continent of Africa who are lucky to hit fifty (twenty is more normal). The worldwide average is 102.5 pounds per year.[4]

Now, I love a good BLT as much as the next girl, but living so high on the hog has a cost, and not just to our wallets. It has an impact on our waistlines, and healthcare system, and world. A quick example: according to the *Journal of Animal Science*, it takes 6.7 pounds of grain and forage, 52.8 gallons of water, 74.5 square feet of farmland, and 1,036 Btus of fossil fuel energy to produce *one quarter pound* of ground beef.[5] No wonder the stuff is so expensive! Meat gobbles more resources than anything else we fill our stomachs with. And that's not even considering the ethical implications of factory farming, genetically engineered livestock, and the stuff we pump into those critters to increase production and keep them healthy in less-than-ideal conditions.

None of this means that we shouldn't eat meat, but we *should* be conscientious about our consumption. Try cutting back. If you come from a meat-and-potatoes family, this may require some adjustments and involve some whining, but it can be done. Scour the Internet for tasty international recipes, pad your meals with other sources of protein, and pick up a few vegetarian cookbooks at the thrift store. Ease into it, replacing pot roasts and pork chops with low-meat options a couple times a week. Your husband may not thank you, but his heart will.

Also, pay attention to where the meat you do eat comes from. Since I live in the country, a lot of my friends stock their freezers with venison harvested during hunting season, or they buy meat from local farmers who keep their animals healthy and happy. It's a win for the farmers, the animals, and the consumers. It may be trickier for suburban and urban folks to find sustainable options, but paying more for ethically sourced meat is not a problem if you're eating less of it.

Consider the cost of meat, and consume it accordingly. It could make a world of difference.

Stewarding Our Finances in Ways That Help Others

By Heidi Wheeler

Our family, which includes four kids age six and under, is living in the tension of what it means to be God-focused with our finances. We're a work in progress, committed to both refraining from and spending money with the intention of being wise stewards.

We definitely don't have all the answers. If anything, we're constantly asking questions, having conversations, and challenging ourselves. How can we spend less to have more available to share? What are creative ways we can use money to bless those in our community and beyond? How can we teach our kids to become focused on others when we have so much?

We're not taking radical measures of self-denial, but purposeful reduction in spending leads to more resources. Cutting back in our home has included things like canceling cable, finding the least-expensive insurance and phone plans, meal planning and using store discounts to save on groceries, limiting Christmas and birthday gifts, and buying a no-frills, used minivan when we needed a new car. In general, we try to live below our means in order to be able to give generously.

Spending takes our mission into account. Purchasing a home was done with hospitality in mind, with space for small groups, house concerts, or a place of safety and warmth for anyone who needs it. We set aside a monthly amount in our budget we label as "kingdom work." Different than a tithe, this money is for things that don't get a tax deduction but do show love and care for others.

Perhaps we can provide a child in the community with a winter coat, treat a discouraged pastor to dinner out, surprise a missionary family with a care package, or cover a Christian conference fee for a friend who is struggling to make ends meet.

Diapers, kids' activity fees, and looming college educations are enough to make any of us feel anxious about meeting our own families' needs. However, creativity allows room for a spectrum of household incomes to harness money for the good of others. It may mean selling unused homeschooling materials to buy a gas card for the family of a patient hospitalized far away. Or hosting a garage sale on behalf of a family raising funds for full-time missions work. Offering free childcare to a friend who is willing to work extra hours and donate those funds is a creative way to make financial resources go to good things.

As his people seek to use money as a tool for expanding God's purposes, he brings kingdom perspective and freedom from the culture's approach—one that can be passed down to the next generation. It definitely will change the family dinner conversations. I recently overheard this between siblings: "Some kids have to drink water that animals went potty in. That's sad, huh?"

The discussion quickly turned into a brainstorming session about how to raise money for clean water. So if you see a lemonade stand anytime soon with some excited kids flagging you down—you might want to stop by. There are no limits to the good your spare change may do!

Heidi Wheeler loves to be in community with other women, mutually encouraging each other to health and wholeness of mind, body, and spirit. She's a busy mom of four young children, works part-time using her nurse practitioner training, and writes whenever she can sneak a free moment. She is a contributor for the MKE Moms Blog and a member of Redbud Writer's Guild, and her work can be found at Today's Christian Woman, inCourage, The Mudroom, *and her blog,* TheBlessedNest.com.

Buy a Cow (or a Goat, or Chickens)

If you want to change the world, buy a cow, or a goat, or some chickens. No, I'm not telling you to start a farm (although if you want to, this country girl won't judge). I'm telling you to help someone else start a farm.

Maybe it's my rural roots showing, but I have a soft spot for agricultural aid. Providing livestock through programs like Heifer International or World Vision is a fun, tangible, and relatively inexpensive way to help people in need develop a sustainable source of food and income. What's more, animals multiply, and people who have received the gift pass it on to others in their community.

If you're an animal lover horrified by the thought of providing animals for slaughter, don't flip the page quite yet. Many of these organizations provide the option of donating fruit trees or hardy seed. Alpacas provide families with warm clothes, transportation, and an extra source of income, and yaks are more useful as milk-producing beasts of burden than they are as hamburger. My sister-in-law, a staunch vegetarian who hasn't touched meat in over twenty years, is fond of donating hives of honeybees. They improve pollination while providing struggling farmers with an extra source of income, and she's helping build up the declining honeybee population. Win-win-win.

One of my favorite ways to engage in agricultural aid is to make a donation on someone's behalf as a gift. Most organizations will send the recipient a card via email or snail mail with your message, a picture of the animal you've donated, and sometimes a small plush toy. Imagine sending your niece bunnies on Easter, getting a beehive for your honey on Valentine's Day, or sending your dad an "old goat" on his birthday (as long as he's got a good sense of humor). Word to the wise, though: if you're going to make a donation on a child's behalf, please make sure they get something tangible to go along with it, whether that's a plush toy from the organization itself, another fun gift, or a stocking full of dollar store goodies. Birthdays and holidays are *not* the times to teach children the importance of charity by playing the dour, puritanical Grinch. They'll learn something about your priorities, all right, but probably not what you hoped.

Kids *do* love looking through Heifer catalogs, though, and get excited about the ways animals can change lives. Help your kids brainstorm ways to come up with money to make donations themselves. Could they rake the neighbor's lawn, sell those pot holders they're obsessed with making to some sweet souls at church, or give a percentage of their birthday money to a good cause? I once offered my kids twenty-five cents for every toy they let me give away; it wasn't my proudest parenting moment, but I was desperate to declutter, and at least some of that money went to causes my kids cared about.

So hop online, order a catalog, and indulge in some fantasy farming. It will reap very real benefit for families around the globe.

Quit Coloring Your Hair

There's this episode of *Dr. Who* where the Doctor tells Britain's prime minister, Harriet Jones, that he can bring her government down with six words: "Don't you think she looks tired?"

It's a staggering cultural commentary. It might have gone over my head in my twenties, but now that I'm pushing forty, I totally get it. I had a similar thought looking at myself in the mirror today as I was trying on a new shirt under Goodwill's harsh fluorescent lights. "Oh, Jenny. You look tired." My thoughts immediately went to eyeliner, blush, and blonde highlights, because who wants to listen to a haggard, middle-aged woman?

The underlying message? You're not good enough as you are. Your hair needs lightening. Your skin needs coloring. Your eyes need brightening. Or you're going to be dismissed as frumpy and irrelevant, one of those women everyone ignores instead of admires.

Gross. But we've all fallen prey to that siren song a time or two, haven't we?

So. About hair color.

I remember walking out of a hair salon ten years ago, plunking down nearly $100 for my cut and color, and thinking "This is for the birds." I had paid someone $100 to paint blonde streaks onto my head? Surely God had better uses for that money.

But what really struck me, once the highlights had grown out and I was left with my natural used-to-be-blonde-but-darkened-to-some-indefinable-shade-of-blah hair was how strong the urge was to color it. To cover it. To go beach blonde, or bright red, or bold brunette, or anything other than what it actually was.

This made me suspicious. I began paying closer attention to the women around me, and sure enough, more than half of them had colored their hair (the other half either left it natural or had very good stylists). It looked great on some of them, brightening up their appearance and drawing attention to their face. But others had obviously just colored it to color it, to cover grey or change the shade. They didn't necessarily look better for it, and some of them looked worse. Coloring their hair was more of a compulsion than anything; some of the ladies I talked to had been coloring their hair for so long that they didn't even know what their natural hair looked like anymore.

Is it just me, or does that seem somewhat neurotic?

Now, there's nothing wrong with coloring your hair, so please don't hear me say that there is. I may give into the urge myself someday. But I would really encourage you to think about *why* you want to color your hair, what you get out of coloring it, and how you would feel if you didn't. Make the decision consciously, not just because you gave in to the siren song of modern advertising, or the everyone-else-is-doing-it phenomenon we thought we outgrew after high school. Then, if you still want to color it, go for it! But maybe, just maybe, coming to peace with the hair God gave you will be worth more than anything you save on dye or salon fees.

Let the Buyer Beware

As the economy has become increasingly global, stewarding our finances has become more complex. Here are a few common pitfalls to avoid and ways to make your money count.

ON BUYING CHEAP STUFF

Everyone loves getting a good deal, but the cost of that five-dollar tee shirt may be far higher than you ever imagined. Let's just be honest. The price of many of the goods we rely on is artificially low; we only get them so cheap because people in other parts of the world are slaving away in sweatshops for a couple dollars per day. Some are literally enslaved; if you're looking to kick your chocolate or coffee habit, do some research on the use of child labor in those industries. That'll make you lose your appetite right quick.

Trafficking and child labor aside, it's not all bad news. Manufacturing jobs do create genuine opportunity around the world, and many of our ancestors worked in similar conditions at the end of the nineteenth century and the beginning of the twentieth (which is why they risked their necks organizing labor unions, and why your great-grandpa was so much more liberal than you). But there is a limit, and the money God gave us to manage shouldn't be thrown at companies that take advantage of their workers, just because Johnny needs another pair of cheap shoes.

ON BUYING EXPENSIVE STUFF

So, the answer to that problem is to buy pricey, socially conscious stuff from Christian-owned companies, right? WRONG. Well, maybe not completely wrong. But mostly wrong.

Let's think this through for a minute. Say you want a new purse. You could go to your favorite store and buy a cheaply manufactured one for, say, thirty dollars. But being an ethical consumer, you attend a vaguely Christian Not-Tupperware party, and buy one for sixty dollars instead. Either option is fine, if you really fall in love with a particular purse. But if your primary goal is to make kingdom-conscious purchasing decisions, you'd be better off finding a cute bag at the Salvation Army and donating the difference to a trusted charity.

There are times to spend more. Limiting yourself to fair trade coffee and chocolate is a good example. But generally, it's better to spend less and donate the difference in cash.

ON CHECKING OUT A CHARITY

Just because a company has nonprofit status doesn't mean they manage their resources for maximum impact. Nowadays, it's easy to get information about a charity's transparency, accountability, and use of funds. Do a little digging before you write out that check or hand over your credit card number. On the flip side, don't jump on the bandwagon when people start grabbing their pitchforks and yelling about an NGO's salaries, administrative costs, or hiring practices. Charity work is complicated, especially if the organization operates across international borders, and outrage perpetuated by a lack of understanding has hurt a lot of vulnerable people. Don't get swept up in the propaganda for or against certain organizations; just do your homework, and funnel your dollars to the organization you believe will make the most difference.

Because They Said So!

Bright Ideas from Mentor Moms

We have a general rule: if you need new clothes (and with three kids, we do every season), look secondhand first. Buying new is expensive, and it's often hard to figure out who made the clothes or shoes we buy from retailers; buying secondhand helps us support the local ministries that run the shops. When we can't buy secondhand, we check BetterWorldShopper.org to check out sustainable options.
—Erin F. Wasinger, mama of three

Let your wallet serve as a reminder of your financial priorities. Use a marker to draw a meaningful symbol on the outside of your wallet (a Bible reference or the shape of a country you want to have an impact on would work well), or tuck a thin cross pendant into the clear pocket meant for your driver's license. Scribble something about a cause you care about onto a Post-It note and wrap it around your credit card, taking it off and on every time you spend. When a friend in ministry confided that she was in pain because she couldn't afford a dental procedure, I scribbled "wisdom teeth" on a scrap of paper and kept it in my wallet for months, reminding me to save money to contribute toward her needs. Having a tangible reminder of your priorities in your wallet is a powerful defense against impulse spending.
—Jenny Rae Armstrong, mama of four

My daughters really enjoyed holding a garage sale when I suggested that they could use the proceeds from whatever they sold of theirs to "buy" an item out of the Samaritan's Purse catalog. One daughter had enough to donate baby chicks, my athlete donated soccer balls, and I had enough to fund a goat for a family. It was so much more satisfying than just selling our stuff.
—Lara Seman Krupika, mama of two

I love to find meaningful gifts for friends and family. The mall overwhelms me with the mass marketing and nearly identical items in all the stores, but many alternative options now exist from nonprofits who sell handicrafts online. I get to share a story with my gift giving, the unique gifts are well received, and a crafter in a rural village far away gains money to buy food for her family.
    —Sharon R. Hoover, mama of two

We always go over our giving numbers in December and compare them to our income. Then we make up the gap between our regular giving total and a tithe (10 percent) in larger one-time gifts. It is one of my favorite times of year: to write those big checks and surprise missionaries and our favorite ministries with a year-end boost.
    —Lara Seman Krupika, mama of two

I fight human trafficking by making sure to buy fair trade chocolate and coffee. I also buy fair trade accessories through groups like Trades of Hope.
    —Leah Everson, mama of two

Don't fall into the trap of running to the store several times a week. Marketers are smart people, and stores are set up to entice you into spending money. Make a list of the things you need, get in and out of the store as quickly as possible, and try to go no more than once per week. Many of the rural people where I live go two weeks between shopping trips—stocking the pantry is almost a strategy game for them! If shopping is a form of entertainment to you, make a list of other things you could do for fun—a trip to the library, coffee with a friend, a walk through the nature preserve. Better to spend fifty dollars taking your kids to the children's museum—or the zoo, or to open swim at the Y—than blowing one hundred dollars at Target just because you were bored.
    —Jenny Rae Armstrong, mama of four

Let yourself run out of things. To some extent, our overconsumption is fear-based. We're afraid that if we don't have the things we've always had,

or the security we've always had, we'll just downright fall apart. But even something as simple as allowing yourself to run out of lunch bags—those plastic bags that we use to pack lunches—and finding out what you use, or how you eat differently, can be enlightening.
    —Esther Emery, mama of three

Notes

[1] Anup Shah, "Poverty Facts and Stats," last modified January 17, 2013, www
.globalissues.org/article/26/poverty-facts-and-stats.

[2] "Marketing to Women Quick Facts," *She-conomy,* http://she-conomy.com
/report/marketing-to-women-quick-facts (accessed October 19, 2015).

[3] Margot Adler, "Behind the Ever-Expanding American Dream House," *NPR,*
July 4, 2006, www.npr.org/templates/story/story.php?storyId=5525283.

[4] Eliza Barclay, "A Nation of Meat Eaters: See How It All Adds Up," *The Salt,*
June 27, 2012, www.npr.org/sections/thesalt/2012/06/27/155527365/visualizing
-a-nation-of-meat-eaters.

[5] Ibid.

POWER OUTLET FOUR

Going Global

I was seven when my family moved to Liberia. I still remember standing at the gate in the airport, clutching my teddy bear and contemplating the journey to come. I wasn't too keen on the idea of leaving the States, but none of the invitations my school friends had extended to live in their tree houses had panned out. Besides, I didn't *really* want my parents to move without me.

If I'm honest, I never liked living in Liberia. Oh, there were parts of it that I loved, but I always wanted to move back home, where I felt safe and secure. And then when we did move back, the United States felt almost as foreign to me as Liberia had! It wasn't until I became an adult that I understood what an incredible gift I had been given, spending so much of my childhood in a different country and culture. Yes, growing up expat comes with the danger of feeling like a perpetual outsider, a cultural chameleon who is never really at home anywhere. On the other hand, you learn to create a home for yourself pretty much anywhere. And oh, the experiences you have!

Jesus' last commandment to his followers was to go out into all the world and make disciples of all nations. It wasn't really subtle. Maybe God has called you to pack up your children and move across town, across the country, or across the world, like my parents did. That possibility shouldn't be shrugged off. But even if your passport is collecting dust while you raise your babies, it's never been easier to make a global impact. You can communicate with people around the world with the click of a mouse. You can donate to disaster relief by typing a few numbers into your phone. You can stay up to date on what is happening thousands of miles away by hopping online. And do you have any idea what I would have given to have Skype and Facebook when we lived in Liberia?

Here's another thing to remember: more and more often, the world is coming to us. It always gobsmacks me to hear Christians complain about immigration—God is dropping the nations into our lap, and we're dropping the ball! We need to overcome our politics and prejudices and pay attention to how God is moving in the movement of people. Human migration has always played a huge part in God's plans and purposes, from the days of Abraham right up to today. Are we making the most of every opportunity to share Christ with people from every tongue and tribe and nation, whether they live across the world or across the street?

Just like Abraham, God has blessed us so that we can be a blessing to others. Going global may pull us out of our comfort zone, but I promise you, it will be the adventure of a lifetime. Besides, no matter how appealing staying put in a friend's tree house may sound, you really don't want your Father moving on without you. Hug your teddy bear tight if you must, but let's get moving!

Sponsor a Child

You're probably familiar with this idea. For less than the price of your morning cup of coffee, you can make sure one child in the developing world gets food, medical care, a good education, and a chance to learn about Jesus. Usually, you'll get a picture of your sponsored child and information about him or her, and you can correspond with them through the organization you choose.

Child sponsorship is a great way to get involved in making an impact in one person's life. It's also a wonderful, tangible way to teach your children about giving and to stretch their worldview.

While I was growing up, pictures of two teenage boys lived on our fridge. One was our family's sponsored child through Compassion International, a sweet young man with mild disabilities who had struggled to find a sponsor through the normal channels. The other was a teenage artist my parents had met on the streets of Haiti and decided to take under their wing, sending him art supplies to support his entrepreneurial efforts and wiring tuition money directly to the schools he attended. That kid was sharp as a tack, and they supported him from elementary school all the way through college, launching him into a career in journalism and education.

My parents talked about these two boys constantly, to the point that when I was little, I thought they were adopted brothers, living far away. I learned about Haiti as I learned about them, learned how different life was for people who lived there, and how materially blessed we were in the United States. I learned that there were brilliant young artists living in slums and studying diligently beneath street lights, because there was no electricity in their homes, and disabled children who would slip through the cracks if someone didn't step up to help them. And most importantly, I learned what a blessing and privilege it is to share what we have with people who are less fortunate, even if we don't have much ourselves.

There is no question that my parents changed those boys' lives. But sponsoring those boys changed my life as well, shaping my worldview and informing my earliest understandings of missions, giving, and flat-out human decency.

Consider sponsoring a child through an organization like World Vision or Compassion, or through connections you have with smaller, grassroots ministries overseas. You could choose to sponsor children exactly the same age as yours, or opt to sponsor teens, who are particularly vulnerable and have a hard time finding sponsors. You could focus in on children with special needs, or orphans living in a children's home, or adolescent girls who need to attend a boarding school if they are to have any hope for a future. Whatever you choose, talk to your children about it, explaining why what you are doing is important. Put your sponsored child's picture on the fridge, and encourage your children to write letters or draw pictures for them. Study up on the place your sponsored child lives, pray for them with your kids, and talk about them often, remembering to focus on their dignity and the hard work they do at home and at school, instead of portraying them as some poor charity case. (All children are charity cases, dependent on someone else's support, right? That's how God made it!)

Yes, sponsorship will change the lives of the children you sponsor. But it just might change your children's lives as well, if you let it.

Increase Your Children's Cultural Exposure

"Mom, can we get some of those Chinese french fries?"

I craned my neck to get a glimpse of my kindergartner, buckled securely into his booster seat. "Chinese french fries?"

"You know, those waffle ones?"

The light went on as I recalled the waffle fries at the Chinese buffet we had been to recently. My first response was mortification. How was it that I had grown up feasting on Lebanese flatbreads, savory Indian sweets, and a never-ending parade of West African stews, and my Midwestern babies couldn't even reason out that waffle fries were not authentic Chinese cuisine? I took a deep breath, reminded myself he was tiny yet, and that you just don't know what you don't know. Besides, at least this wasn't as bad as that time we visited a Liberian church, and his brother expressed his surprise that "everyone was brown."

Yeah. Northern Wisconsin is not the best place for teaching kids about diversity. Or basic cultural geography, for that matter.

One of the great tragedies of the United States is that our melting pot has not melted very well. Oh, I know, people prefer the salad bowl metaphor now—everyone mixing and mingling while retaining their unique cultural flavor. But let's face it. You're still likely to get a mouthful of lettuce, or nothing but tomato, if you plunge your fork into certain areas.

De facto segregation is alive and well, and there is a good chance that your church, your neighborhood, your children's schools, and the businesses you frequent are populated by people who look a whole lot like you. My jaw about hit the floor when I was listening to an NPR broadcast on school segregation and learned that 1988 was the height of desegregation in the United States.[1] 1988! Our babies' schools are less diverse than the ones we attended, and many of you reading this weren't even born when America was at its integrated best.

There is much more that can and should be said about why this is a problem. We should all be nurturing meaningful relationships with people from backgrounds that are different than our own. But exposing our children to a variety of cultures is a baby step in the right direction. Granted, this is easier in urban areas, but even backwoods country folk like me can find ways to make it happen.

Expose your kids to different cuisine, and talk about the cultural background of the foods you are eating. Take a tour of a synagogue or mosque, or go to a concert featuring another nation's folk music. Shop at an ethnic grocery store. Read your kids stories starring children from different places and races. Practice origami together, or learn how to write the Arabic alphabet. Play games from different cultures, or learn how to say "I love you" in as many languages as possible. And, of course, do your very best to help your children cultivate relationships with people from different cultures, whether those cultures are inside or outside the United States.

Breaking out of our cultural ghettos is going to require some thought and intentionality, but do what you need to do to increase your children's cultural exposure. Even if it's as simple as taking them out for "Chinese french fries."

Get Involved With International Students at the University

Moving away for college is a challenging time for everyone. You have to make new friends, adjust to new expectations, and learn to manage your life without your parents' direct guidance. A huge number of college freshmen drop out after the first semester, and the number one reason they cite is loneliness.

Now imagine that on top of all that, you've been given the thrilling opportunity to study in a different country—America! Your family has made huge sacrifices to make this happen, and has high expectations of what you will accomplish. There's a lot riding on your success. But your English skills, which seemed stellar at your local high school, are stretched to the breaking point as you try to understand the professor's heady lectures. Your classmates are even harder to decipher, with their rapid-fire speech and unfamiliar lingo. The culture is confusing, and your fellow students don't seem particularly interested in getting to know you or taking the time to develop a meaningful relationship with someone from such a different context. Even when you are invited to social activities, you feel like the token foreigner—a curiosity to be studied by tipsy sorority girls who ask you to "say something in African," not a person to be related to on a deep level. When the other students go home for Christmas, holiday weekends, and spring break, you have nowhere to go, so you stay in the dorms, eating food service and studying.

It can be incredibly isolating and lonely.

Getting involved with international students at your local university is a great way to have an impact on someone's life. Unlike foreign exchange programs, host families for international college students don't typically invite the students to live with them. Instead, they function as caring mentors and friends who can help the students navigate the culture. Many host families have the students over for meals every now and then, take them shopping for climate-appropriate clothing, and invite them home for the holidays. The students enjoy getting out of the dorms and into a home environment, where they can interact with a regular family. Having kids is a bonus, not a detriment; many students have younger siblings, cousins, or neighbors back home, and miss interacting with children.

Some students may be interested in visiting your church or learning more about Christianity. This is not something that you should pressure them about, particularly since they may worry that your friendship hinges on their participation, or come from a culture where refusing an invitation outright would be rude. But you can certainly let them know that they would be welcome to join you for church, and issue special invitations to holiday services that are both religious and cultural events. And, hopefully, you talk about your faith as a regular course of life. (Check out the Bright Ideas "Tell Your Story" and "Tell God's Story" if talking about your faith is difficult for you.) Many international students have met Jesus during the course of their studies in the States and returned to their home cultures to share Christ in places where Western missionaries are neither effective nor allowed.

Contact the university nearest you to learn how you can get involved with the international students who study there. If they don't have any formal programs, connect with campus ministries such as InterVarsity or Cru to find out how they are reaching out to international students and how you could help. You don't need to travel the world to reach the world for Christ. The world has already traveled to your local university.

"Adopt" a Missionary Kid

Did you know that I'm famous? At least, I'm famous in church circles in northwestern Wisconsin. As a missionary kid (MK), my face was plastered on church bulletin boards and crowded refrigerators all over the county, thanks to the annual family photo reminding people to pray for their missionaries. Decades later, I'm still recognized by random people around town, even without the braids, sundress, and Coppertone tan.

But no matter how many people knew my face, few knew what was going on behind those wide blue eyes and demure smile. And oh, did I resent that!

Missionary kids experience a tremendous amount of loss in their young lives. Loss of family, friends, home, pets, cultural identity, and the special toys and stuffed animals that make them feel secure. While it's becoming less common, many of these precious children still spend their tender years in boarding schools far from their parents and siblings. And because mission work tends to be idealized by churches and Christian culture, MKs who struggle with the sacrifices they are forced to make in the name of God are often not taken seriously or, worse, are treated like they are rebelling against God and the work he wants to do through their parents.

Tearful, traumatized children don't look good on people's refrigerators. Buck up, or people will stop sending your parents money, and all your friends will go to hell!

Oh, I want to weep for these precious children! The stakes are high, and the consequences are eternal. But the good news is, you can help.

Many people commit to pray for and support missionaries. Why not do the same for missionary kids? Pray for them, send them letters or postcards, and encourage your kids to be pen pals. Staying in contact gives MKs a touch point with their home culture and relationships to pick up when they return.

Sending packages overseas is expensive, but if you can swing it, it's a great way to lift an MK's spirits. My Grandma Irma would send VHS tapes of *Reading Rainbow*, *The Smurfs*, and the Disney Sunday night specials we used to watch together. Once she sent pressed wildflowers from her yard—I cherished them for years and would take them out and touch the petals whenever I got especially homesick. At Christmas and on my birthday, my church would send a package stuffed with glittery, handmade cards from my old Sunday school friends. I loved it! And one lady from church—my grandma's best friend, Skip—made a point of sending me letters, postcards, and little gifts until the day I moved back to Wisconsin as an adult. Skip passed away several years ago, but she is still my hero.

Mission work is incredibly important, but so are the children of those called to serve overseas. "Adopt" a missionary kid, and make sure they know they are important to you too.

Buy a Bicycle

"Let me tell you what I think about bicycling.
I think it has done more to emancipate women
than anything else in the world."

—Susan B. Anthony

Ah, bicycles. For most of us, they are a symbol of childhood—a rite of passage, a Christmas wish, a piggy bank full of babysitting money to upgrade to a shinier model. But when they first came out, and women began riding them, bicycles became a symbol of empowerment and even subversion. A woman on a bicycle was going places, and not everyone liked that. In 1896, *Munsey's Magazine* published an article on the topic, explaining that "to men, the bicycle in the beginning was merely a new toy . . . To women, it was a steed upon which they rode into a new world."[2]

To most of us in the Western world, the bicycle is merely a toy. But to people in the developing world, it is *still* a steed upon which they can ride into a new world. Bicycles transform lives, futures, and entire communities. What's more, sturdy bicycles can go places cars can't, improving mobility for people living or working in the most inaccessible, far-flung reaches of the earth.

Think about it. Children who ride bicycles to school instead of walking have more time left over to study and are less likely to be harassed or assaulted along the way, making them particularly important for girls. Women on bicycles can gather water for drinking, cooking, and cleaning in far less time, and men can carry more wares to market when they are hitched to a bike, instead of lugged on their backs. A healthcare worker can visit four times as many patients when they're traveling by bike instead of by foot, and local pastors can carry the gospel further when they've got a set of wheels under them.

Bicycles are transformative. Bicycles are empowering. Bicycles are subversive, in the best possible way.

Plus, I can almost guarantee you that your kids will think donating a bicycle is the coolest idea ever.

There are many different ways you can provide bikes for people in the developing world. World Vision takes monetary donations to buy bikes for schoolgirls, and Gospel for Asia has a similar program for indigenous missionaries. Bikes for the World collects used bikes and ships them overseas, and World Bicycle Relief has great ideas for people who want to put on bicycle-focused fundraisers. Many organizations train local entrepreneurs to maintain and repair bicycles, so the bikes stay in good working order while providing someone in the community with a source of income.

Bicycles are even more awesome than you thought when you were a kid, huh? Maybe it's time to bust out that piggy bank again and start saving up for a bicycle.

Pack a Shoebox

Who doesn't love presents? Operation Christmas Child, a ministry of Samaritan's Purse, is a fun way to help your children engage while spreading Christmas cheer, and the message of God's love, to children around the world. Shoeboxes full of fun gifts are collected at over four thousand locations around the United States, then shipped around the world. Samaritan's Purse partners with local churches to get the presents to the kids, along with a kid-friendly booklet explaining the gospel in their own language.

In my experience, kids love packing shoeboxes almost as much as receiving them. Since you can choose the gender and age range your gift is meant for, I have generally let my sons choose the gifts (with a little direction) and pack a box for a boy about their age. Here are a couple of tips for packing a great shoebox:

CHOOSE YOUR CONTAINER

You can order or pick up an Operation Christmas Child box, or you could use any old shoebox you have around the house. If you are going to wrap the gift, make sure the top is wrapped separately, so it can be opened and closed without destroying the decoration. Personally, I prefer to send sturdy plastic shoeboxes with snap-on lids. (Make sure you don't buy the cheap dollar-store variety. They're too brittle and get decimated in shipping.) They're only a couple bucks and they're incredibly useful. You could buy a colored box or line the inside of a clear one with wrapping paper if you want it to look festive.

FILL IT UP

Samaritan's Purse suggests sending one "wow" gift, such as a soccer ball and pump or a doll (light brown skin is the most universal), and then filling in the space with other fun items. Jump ropes, sunglasses, balls, and flashlights are always a hit. Include school supplies and hygiene items as well, but remember: it's a present. If your child would be disappointed opening the gift on Christmas morning, reconsider. Pray for the child who will be receiving the gift as you pack it, and consider including a family photo and a little note or card.

KEEP IT OUT

Don't send any liquids, lotions, or aerosols, and avoid packing things that could break. Don't send anything that could melt, like chocolate. Toy weapons or military figures are an absolute no-no—some of these kids live in places that have been ravaged by war, and they don't need the trauma of opening a present and finding something that stirs up frightening memories. Neither do their mamas. Be circumspect about animal toys. Animals often carry cultural significance (think about our associations regarding bats or black cats), and while your son may think his rubber snake is awesome, kids who have to watch out for venomous reptiles may find them less amusing. Stick with simple, sturdy, easy-to-use playthings, fun accessories, and things that would delight your child's heart.

SEND IT OFF

Check online to find out where the nearest collection center is, and what the collection dates are. Make sure that your box is labeled, letting people know which gender and age level it is meant for. You can print a tracking label off the Samaritan's Purse website, and they will send you information about where your box winds up. Don't forget to include a check, or to make the suggested donation online, to help with the cost of shipping and distribution. Have fun with it!

Eat Like the Rest of the World Once a Week

Looking for a delicious way to raise your kids' awareness? Once a week, serve your family a simple evening meal that reflects how the rest of the world eats. Then send the money you save to a feeding program or agricultural charity, like Food for the Hungry or Heifer International. A pot of rice and beans only costs a couple dollars, so if you usually spend ten to fifteen dollars per meal, you could scrounge up forty bucks or so per month. Plus, your kids get a tangible lesson on what life is like in the rest of the world.

Whatever you do, though, don't turn the evening into a first-world guilt fest, complete with shaming rants about how "children are starving in ——————————" (fill in the blank), so your children are horrible people if they don't eat their peas. Just don't. Make the meal fun for your family, something your kids look forward to each week! Whip out a map or your copy of *Operation World*, pick a country, and set a theme. Let the kids make decorations. Put pillows on the floor and eat around your coffee table by the light of a kerosene lamp. And for goodness sake, if your family can't stand black bean curry or legume stew, let them enjoy PB&Js while you read them the Uzbek folktale you found online, or listen to Kenyan tunes on Pandora.

If you want to try the rice and beans thing, here's a kid-friendly recipe that my family loves.

1 can corn, drained
1 can black beans, drained and rinsed
1 16 oz. jar of mild salsa

Two cups shredded cooked chicken (You can replace the chicken with two cups of cooked rice if you prefer a vegetarian option.)

Mix the ingredients; warm them up with the stove, microwave, or Crock-Pot; and voila! A cheap, healthy, and kid-friendly concoction that can be served over rice, wrapped in a tortilla, or scooped up with chips. Sour cream and cheese make it extra yummy.

As you can see, this is not about creating an authentic cultural experience. It's about building curiosity, interest, and empathy in your children, and saving a few bucks on your grocery bill so you can pass the blessing of a full plate to brothers and sisters on the other side of the global table. Have fun with it!

Become Host Parents

By Jen Underwood

I said it casually, just dropped it into the conversation my husband and I were having about the latest news at the Christian school where we both taught. "You know, two of the international students still don't have a host family for the school year."

My husband nodded and then said, "Yeah, I've been thinking about that. Praying about it, actually."

I had too. And that's how we began host parenting four years ago. I was a bit terrified at first. After all, for ten months we would have two relative strangers living with us, not just as boarders, but, in a way, as our "kids." We would have to navigate personality differences, general likes and dislikes, and the sharing of bathrooms and a kitchen with cultural challenges as well.

But I was also excited to expand our family's world. My husband and I had taught in Okinawa, Japan, before our first child was born, and discovered we loved being in a different culture and working with students from around the world. Even after we returned to the States and had children, we continued to visit different countries; in fact, our youngest was adopted as a result of a trip to a child sponsorship program in Uganda. We think it's really important for our family to remember that God's world extends far beyond our suburb, and we do a lot to keep stretching our kids' cultural comfort zones. We knew host parenting would bring someone else's world into our very home.

We were also excited about the impact we hoped to make on our students' lives. Many of the students in our school's international program are not Christ-followers and do not come from

Christian backgrounds. Their parents agree to their placement in Christian homes and their attending church. One of the host parents in our program is fond of saying "God has brought our mission field to us!" It's true. For ten months, our students watch how we live in the intimacy of our families. That can be really powerful! They watch as we try to love as Christ loves; they watch as we mess up; they watch as we apologize and ask for forgiveness.

This last lesson—of forgiveness—has had incredible impact. I remember the first time I messed up in front of one of our international students. I'd yelled at one of my children, and I was sure I'd destroyed our testimony to this girl who had never had real interaction with Christians before. But the Holy Spirit prompted me to make my confession to my child just as public as my yelling, and my child forgave me in front of our international student. At the end of the year, when this student thanked me for hosting her, she told me she'd been impressed by the forgiveness in our family—both for each other and for her. "You loved even after someone made a mistake," she said, "and you kept loving me even when I wasn't easy to love."

The number of international high school students in the United States continues to grow each year. Some (more than 20,000) come through an exchange program, but approximately 50,000 others come seeking a diploma, meaning they will attend a U.S. high school for an entire school year or multiple years. More than 800,000 others are attending college or graduate school.

Does the idea of hosting excite you? Are you willing to share your home, your life, and yourself with a student from another culture? Type the words "hosting international students" into a Web search engine, and you'll get many results. If you would prefer to work with a Christian program, contact your local Christian high school or college and see if it has an international student program. Just think about the global impact Christian families could have through hosting these students—who will in turn have an impact when they return to their cultures that are often relatively untouched by the Christian faith.

"Do not take advantage of foreigners who live among you in your land. Treat them like native-born Israelites, and love them as you love yourself. Remember that you were once foreigners living in the land of Egypt. I am the LORD your God" (Lev. 19:33–34 NLT).

Jen Underwood lives with her husband, their four kids (two girls, two boys), two international high school students (both girls), and a dog in the western suburbs of Chicago. She works as a writer/editor, serves as a ministry leader and teacher at her church, and is a member of the Redbud Writer's Guild. She blogs at jenunderwood.org.

Pray Your Way around the World

Prayer changes things. The debate about whether it changes God's mind, spurring him to action he would not have taken otherwise, will probably go on until we see him face to face. But there is one thing I know for sure: when we pray, the Holy Spirit changes *us*, spurring *us* to take action we might not have taken otherwise. Prayer is dangerous. Beautifully, wildly dangerous. And we have the incredible privilege of teaching our children to pray.

If you're holding this book in your hands, it probably means three things: you love Jesus, you love your children, and you love this heartbreaking world. Prayer is the intersection of these three loves—the spiritual battleground where realities are shaped and destinies are forged, and we join our voices with the voice of Jesus, calling for God's will to be done on earth as it is in heaven. It has an impact on our hearts, our homes, our communities, and our world.

Oftentimes, our prayers for and with our children focus on domestic concerns. Saying grace before meals, praying that we'll find lost toys or that grandma's knee will feel better, or even praying for their future spouse. That's wonderful, but why not teach your children to pray for the really big stuff too? Why not teach your children to pray that God will change the world?

If you have friends, relatives, or missionaries you support who live in different countries, or if your children know people who have lived in different countries, that's a good place to start. Research those places with your children. What are some interesting facts about the culture, the climate, the language, the history? What is especially good about it? What do the people struggle with? What is there to be thankful for, and what do they need? Then, pray with your children, asking God to act on what you have learned. Stay connected, continuing to learn and pray with your children as you wait and watch expectantly for answers to prayer.

If you aren't sure where to start, or want to expose your child to a wide variety of cultures, check out *Window on the World* by Daphne Spraggett and Jill Johnstone. It's basically *Operation World* for kids: a colorful, informative prayer guide to a variety of nations and people groups. It is pretty old-school and may need some clarification and updating, but it is still a great jumping-off point for learning about different cultures and how to pray for them. Consider reading about and praying for one culture per week.

Or you can split the difference and see whether your church or denomination puts out a prayer guide or prayer calendar for the missionaries they support. These will often provide little snippets of information about the missionaries themselves, the contexts they are serving in, and particular prayer concerns. One of the benefits of using a denominational guide is that there are more opportunities to connect with the missionaries in person or through correspondence. And I can assure you, missionaries love getting notes letting them know that people are praying for them—that a whole family has committed to praying for their family.

Prayer is one of the ways in which God forms us. If we want to change the world, let's begin by praying for it and teaching our children to pray for it as well. Who knows? Perhaps God will change the world by changing us.

Because They Said So!

Bright Ideas from Mentor Moms

My son and I have sponsored a little girl in Uganda for several years. She is exactly his age, and we exchange letters and pictures almost every month. We pray for each other. My son and I study Africa and quiz my brother, who has traveled there, and try to remember how differently most of the world lives.
—Natalie Nyquist, mama of one

Visit an immigrant church regularly. I've been at mine for the past two years and have gotten to know brothers and sisters in Christ from all over Latin America. I've been astonished at how different the preaching is—there's much more of a global focus and more attention to issues facing people of color, and the congregation is more conservative than mine theologically. There's almost always someone available to translate, but sitting in a service where you're lost is an eye-opening experience—one I wish more people who are not bilingual would experience.
—Heather Caliri, mama of two

One way to raise global kids in a global world is to provide opportunities for kids to be bilingual (ideally, trilingual). Early language immersion is important for establishing the skills kids need to thrive in our global world. I chose a childcare provider who is Ethiopian so my little one would be exposed to another language and culture. At two, he eats kocho, and my mom says he speaks Amharic!
—Lorie Lee, mama of one

Get on a plane and go! Yes, there is a lot of financial, logistical, and emotional work involved in international travel, especially if you're not accustomed to it, but there is nothing that can compare to experiencing

another culture firsthand. Go on a mission trip, fly out to visit a ministry your church supports, or take a trip to see friends overseas. It's an eye-opening experience that just may change your life.
—Jenny Rae Armstrong, mama of four

Invite visiting missionaries into your home. This is something we have always done, as my very hospitable parents did as I was growing up, and it has made a huge impact. Then keeping in touch, visiting abroad, and supporting those who you've had around your family table makes missions personal and important for children. Hearing what God is doing across the world helps them to become more global, missional thinkers.
—Terri Kraus, mama of one

We are on the board of the Missionary Furlough Homes Foundation, which provides housing for missionaries here on furlough. Our kids have had a large part in preparing the house we take care of and meeting the missionaries who stay in the house for a year. It's been a fantastic way to expose the kids to missions work without leaving home. Also, when our kids were very young, we saved frequent flier miles forever so that we could take them to Brazil to visit missionary friends there.
—Shelly Wildman, mama of three

Grow your children's cultural awareness by combining reading with food. One summer I gave my kids the choice of going to an Ethiopian, Cambodian, or Afghan restaurant in town if they read a corresponding book about those countries: The Storyteller's Beads, The Clay Marble, *or* Parvana's Journey. *They chose Ethiopian because they could eat with their hands, and we had a blast.*
—Beth Bruno, mama of three

Notes

[1] "The Problem We All Live With," narrated by Ira Glass, *This American Life*, *NPR*, July 31, 2015, www.thisamericanlife.org/radio-archives/episode/562/the-problem-we-all-live-with.

[2] Joseph Stromberg, "'Bicycle Face': A 19th Century Health Problem Made Up to Scare Women Away from Biking," *Vox*, last updated March 24, 2015, www.vox.com/2014/7/8/5880931/the-19th-century-health-scare-that-told-women-to-worry-about-bicycle.

POWER OUTLET FIVE

Mommy on a Mission

I lay in my rumpled bed, exhausted but impressed. Baby number four wasn't even three months old yet, but the articulation of the sobs wafting from his crib seemed too clear to be coincidence.

"Ma-ma-ma-ma-ma!"

I stumbled out of bed for another midnight milk-and-snuggle-fest.

Mothers play a unique role in a child's spiritual development. From birth and even before, we learn about God's provision, compassion, and fierce, protective love from the women he placed in our lives to carry, nourish, nurture, and shelter us. From an infant's perspective, mommy is the source of everything they need (a fact that can be annoying when you begin to feel like a human binky, but is nonetheless incredibly significant). Of course, human mothers fall short of the heavenly ideal they point toward, but every heart is hardwired to yearn for the unfailing love we associate with mothers: a love only God can fully supply.

Parenting is a sobering proposition. As busy and successful as we may become in other areas of our lives, and as much as others may seem to need us, a company can always get a new employee; an organization, a new volunteer. But mothers and fathers aren't so easily replaced. We need to keep that in mind as we organize our schedules and our priorities. Besides, while it's almost impossible to believe when you're drowning in diapers and burp cloths, this intensive phase of parenting doesn't last forever. As my husband is fond of saying, "I'm looking forward to missing these days."

As suffocating as the early years of motherhood may feel, they also offer access to amazing ministry opportunities. Seriously! It would look pretty weird if I showed up at a playgroup or parenting class with my six-foot-something behemoths, but you, still at a stage with small children, can go and connect with mamas who need Jesus. Many women cut back their work hours while their kids are small. And while mommying is certainly a full-time job, spending more time at home provides an element of flexibility that can bless not just your family, but your community. Take advantage of that! As a mother, you've got an automatic in with every grandma who makes eyes at your infant at the bus stop, and every crying kid who's lost in the store. Having a baby in a carrier and two toddlers hanging off you basically screams "I am a safe person!" Talk with people who seem anxious to engage, and pray that God will use your conversation to bless them and draw them closer to him.

There are so many ways we can use our role as mothers to reach out to people who desperately need God's love, both inside and outside our homes. In Christ, you are never "just a mom." You are a mommy on a mission!

Have the Neighbor Kids Over

When I was growing up, playdates were as common as water. In fact, they were so common we didn't have a fancy name like "playdates" to describe them. Sleepovers required permission, but going over to so-and-so's house was just part of what kids did after school and on weekends, as long as it was within walking distance and you were home in time for supper. Of course, that was back in the day of latchkey kids and actual free time, when moms could let their nine-year-olds bike to the park without fear of being arrested for child endangerment. But I digress.

In retrospect, one of the neatest things about the "mi casa es su casa" nature of the neighborhoods I grew up in was that kids developed very comfortable relationships with their friends' parents. Of course, the parents all got to know one another as well, to make sure their kids weren't hanging out with axe murderers, and some kids spent more time at my house than vice versa, based on those findings. But I learned a lot from my friends' parents, from better ways of tying my shoes to how to make my lipstick stay on longer, and I always had a long list of trusted adults I knew I could turn to in a crisis. My friends' parents were influential figures in my life, and my parents were influential in my friends' lives, as well.

I'm not sure when, exactly, the casual neighborhood house-hopping I grew up with became less common, but I think it's a shame. True, parents are working longer hours, kids are involved in more after-school activities, and Pinterest has made us all neurotic, like having the neighbor kids over means we have to bake cute little spring-themed cupcakes and play educational games with them, instead of just chasing them down into the basement and letting them do somersaults on the old couch cushions. But there is such an incredible opportunity here for moms to minister to their neighbors and make a lasting impact on children's lives. We just have to get over ourselves, our fears, and our insecurities, and let the little children come.

If the idea of throwing your doors wide open freaks you out, try taking baby steps toward casual hospitality. If you never have people over, take a deep breath, do whatever you need to do to feel comfortable, and invite a family into your home. If you already have people over from time to time, but not as often as you'd like because of the time it takes to get things "company ready," invite someone over and forbid yourself from cleaning ahead of time. Wring your hands and warn them about the state of your house if you must, but do it! Try setting aside one afternoon a week for your kids to have a friend or two over, and see how it goes. (Make sure that you let them play, instead of taking it upon yourself to entertain them. Weekly birthday-party-esque gatherings are not allowed.) Perhaps you could even offer to watch the neighbor kids for an hour or two after school until their parents get home from work.

Having your kids' friends over doesn't have to be a big deal for you. But it will definitely be a big deal for them, a chance for them to interact with an adult who loves Jesus and cares deeply about them. So whaddaya say, Mom? Can the neighbor kids come over to play?

118

Create Care Packages for Homeless People

"Mom, that person needs help!"

I glanced out the window at the unkempt man on the street corner holding a cardboard sign. It's a rare sight where I live, rare enough that panhandling doesn't have the gloss of invisibility. My kids noticed and were concerned.

I hemmed and hawed about what to tell them. When we lived and worked in town, I'd kept McDonald's gift certificates in the car to share with anyone who needed a meal, a hot cup of coffee, or just a warm place to sit for an hour. But that day, I was completely unprepared. I wound up driving past the man and having a long conversation about it with the kids.

Helping panhandlers and homeless folks can be a complicated proposition. Giving cash (which is all most of us have on hand at any given moment) can do more harm than good, but passing them by sends a message as well, to the person we are ignoring as well as to the little people who are watching our every move. At the very least, we should treat people with courtesy, remembering that they are created in the image of God and dearly loved. But we could do more. Think ahead about how you would like to respond to people asking for help, and get your kids in on the preparations. Here are a few tips:

KNOW THE OPTIONS

What options are available to people in your community who need a shower, a meal, or a warm place to sleep? Do your homework, so you can point people toward organizations that provide both short-term and long-term assistance. Many communities provide cards or pamphlets listing local service providers. Keep a few in your purse, so you can give them to people in need.

DON'T BE CAUGHT EMPTY-HANDED

Keep a few gift certificates or transit cards in your wallet so you can share them with folks who need them. These are nice to have on hand when you are concerned about the teenager loitering in front of the gas station or skulking in a corner of the mall too.

MAKE A CARE PACKAGE

Hit the dollar store with your kids and make some care packages to keep in the car. Warm socks and baby wipes are a great start; a comb, lip balm, sunblock, and Band-Aids are welcome additions. Filling snacks like beef jerky or protein bars are better than anything too sticky or sweet, since dental hygiene is tough for people who live on the streets. Go ahead and add a toothbrush and toothpaste, but avoid mouthwash, hand sanitizer, and anything that contains alcohol. Pop in a Mylar emergency blanket (you can order a lot of these online for pennies apiece, and if you live in a cold climate you should keep a few in your car anyway in case of emergencies). Include a card listing local service agencies, and perhaps a readable version of the New Testament.

Don't be caught empty-handed when people ask you for help! Think ahead so you are able to respond the way you want to.

Stop "Stuff-itis"

I'll never forget the evening I realized how cluttered my home office was. (Well, I call it an office. My mom calls it a closet.) It's a sweet little 8-by-8 space with a built-in desk and these bottle-green vintage shelves that I salvaged from the basement of a former house. My office is a girly retreat from the testosterone-fest that is my house. But the problem with home offices, particularly when they look suspiciously like a walk-in closet, is that they are an incredibly convenient place to shove stuff when company comes over on short notice. But when you step into them later, you are in creative mode, not cleaning mode. So stuff tends to pile up.

It was the trombone that caught my attention. Why was there a trombone in my writing room? Then I noticed the Chicken Dance Ernie (the Sesame Street character, wearing a chicken suit), a hideous pink purse, the printer that hadn't worked in four months, and the preschooler nestled in a sleeping bag under my desk.

Things were out of control. I carried the baby to his bed, grabbed a handful of garbage bags, and began decluttering.

Let's just be honest. The average American household has too much stuff. We spend hours every week (if not every day) managing our stuff, cleaning our stuff, searching for our stuff, fixing our stuff, moving our stuff around to make room for more stuff, all while wishing we had better stuff.

Kids only amplify this problem, and heaven help you if grandparents are in the mix. Christmas alone could disrupt the delicate balance, making a peaceful playroom look like the four horsemen of the apocalypse had swung through after raiding the local Toys"R"Us. The odds are not in your favor.

There's nothing inherently wrong with having stuff. I am personally most comfortable surrounded by books, coffee mugs, and mismatched chairs, so I'm not saying you should go all spartan on your living space. But when your stuff begins to crowd out your mental, emotional, and physical energy, and consumes more time than it saves, it's time to serve your clutter an eviction notice.

So here's a challenge—get rid of the stuff you don't really use and enjoy, and don't rush out to Target or garage sales to fill the empty space with new stuff. Learn to breathe. Learn to live with open spaces in your home, and in your life. Make room for something new—something that God may have for you that you were too busy managing "stuff" to consider before.

If you want to sell your stuff on Craigslist and give the proceeds to charity, more power to you. But if you're like me and just need the stuff gone, simply box it up and bring it directly to the Salvation Army store. They'll do good stuff with the money they make off your stuff, and you won't have to deal with your stuff anymore.

Un-stuff your life, and leave space open for other things. You may feel edgy and insecure at first, but you'll be glad you did.

Foster Parenting and Adoption

By Ellen Stevens

When she first walked through our front door, we had no idea "Ladybug" would change our lives forever. With thick black hair and beautiful olive skin, a forehead that went on for miles and nostrils that flared wide when she laughed, this little squirt never met a stranger; everyone was a friend. But many had no idea what lurked beneath her surface. By day, she was full of life and adventure. At night, bad dreams ravaged her, surfacing the trauma her little heart, mind, and body had endured.

Early one morning, I was enjoying a rare quiet time praying while our foster daughter was careening off the walls in her room. Soon, I sensed I was being watched. I turned to see her squatting, watching me with pensive eyes that had seen far more in six years than they should in a lifetime. Slowly, she crawled over and curled into my arms. I continued praying, recognizing that she was drawn to the peace. We remained on the floor for close to an hour—I, getting lost in God, and she, tucked up in his warm presence. Finally, she tapped me on the leg. "Can you teach my mom to pray like that?"

My heart broke, and I told her that since her mother wasn't around, I would teach Ladybug to pray. I pulled a chair to the corner of the room and told her she could tell God all of her secrets. She sat quiet for a while, and then the hushed sounds began. Slow and cautious soon gave way to waves of whispers, tumbling out of her heart, as tears washed over her rocking body. She had finally met her Father.

After Ladybug returned to her biological mother, three preteen brothers made their way into our home and hearts. After two years

123

of foster care, adopting these boys brought endless life into our world. While we are technically a family of five, we also gained six "nieces and nephews"—their biological siblings, all of whom have also been adopted. As we offer light to our sons, they pass goodness to their siblings, who pass it to their families, who pass it to their communities.

"How can you bring a child into your home knowing they may leave and you'll never see them again?" "I just couldn't say good-bye." "What if they want to go back to their parents?" "Too many memories." "Too many risks."

Becoming a foster parent is more than just one option for entering motherhood or building a family. It is a calling to recognize that the bandage you place on a wobbly scooter rider can heal far more than a skinned knee. It restores a child's heart and moves through them to hopefully, one day, heal their family and your world.

Today, there are approximately 415,000 children in the U.S. foster care system, of whom 132,000 are eligible for adoption. Unfortunately, nearly 33 percent of these children will bounce from home to home for over three years before they are finally welcomed into a forever family.

Making a difference can begin with providing foster children with backpacks of clothing, toiletries, and school supplies; offering brief day or overnight respite for weary foster parents; supporting foster children organizations like the faith-based, volunteer-run Royal Family Kids; or volunteering to represent a child's voice as a court-appointed special advocate.

For some, pursuing foster care of an older kid, sibling group, or special needs child is a gift they can both give and receive. Offering your home and heart to a broken child brings lifelong change to everyone involved.

While my life is now packed with tree forts, race cars, and football games, I still miss Ladybug. Yet I know that for at least one year of her life, she knows she was deeply, profoundly loved. And I know that for the rest of her life, she knows how to find her Father and wrap up into his warm, protective arms.

~~~~~~~~~~~~~~~~~~

Ellen Stevens explores the sacred messiness where faith and life collide at www.ellenstevens.com.

Teach Your Kids the Bible

"Mom, how did the people in Jericho get all those slushies to dump on the children of Israel?"

I looked at my third son, buckled into his booster seat, in consternation. Now, I love VeggieTales as much as the next person. But when your kids' understanding of the Bible is colored by talking peas and giant pickles, it's time to step up your game.

I'm sure some of us have unhappy memories of struggling to memorize Scripture or going over the catechism when we'd rather be playing outside. Others may feel insecure about their ability to teach their children the Bible because they barely understand it themselves. Don't start panicking yet! Teaching your kids about the Bible doesn't have to be a dry, academic burden, and you can learn right alongside them. Here are a couple of ideas to try.

START WITH THE STORIES

Invest in a good book of Bible stories. *Egermeier's Bible Story Book* is the classic, although there are many good options. All Bible storybooks are abridged, of course, but look for one that dives deep into the narrative. If there aren't at least five stories involving Moses and the Israelites in the wilderness, and if you aren't introduced to any of the judges aside from Samson and Samuel or any of the kings aside from David and Solomon, your child is unlikely to learn anything beyond what they'd pick up in Sunday school. Go deeper.

WATCH

Over the years, there have been scores of children's films made about the Bible. *Superbook*. Hanna-Barbera's The Greatest Adventure series. Any number of short and feature length films to pique your children's interest in the Bible. Recently, I've been obsessed with the What's in the Bible series put out by Phil Vischer, the creator of VeggieTales (evidently he ran into that whole "slushy" phenomenon too, and took steps to correct it). Seriously, if you watched that entire series, you'd learn more about the Bible than most people do in a lifetime, and have fun while you're at it. Check it out!

PLAY

When I was little, I loved acting out Bible stories with my mom. My favorite was Mary Magdalene in the garden. I would be Mary and make my mom play the part of Jesus—I'd pretend to cry, we'd go through the dialogue, then I'd gasp and throw my chubby little arms around "Jesus" when I realized who it was. One of the great things about this is that it helps kids put themselves in the biblical character's shoes and contemplate what was going on in them. It may feel awkward or even irreverent to some adults, but if you have little ones who love playing pretend, why not give it a try? Play is how God wired children to learn, after all.

GO HIGH TECH

Is there anything kids nowadays love more than playing on tablets and phones? There are several Bible apps out there made just for children, complete with interactive storybooks, animations, and games that build their biblical knowledge. Download a few and pass your phone to the kids during car rides. It will keep both you and them happy. Win-win!

Stop Pretending to Be Color-Blind

"Look, Mom! Black people! And we're not even in Africa!"

My baby brother was confused. A coup had forced us out of Liberia, the only home he remembered, and back to the glaringly white enclave of northern Wisconsin. Seeing black people where he had assumed there were none blew his four-year-old mind. He was delighted; the rest of us were mortified. My parents apologized to the family, who graciously took it in stride.

We may have the tact not to yell about it in public, but seriously, folks? None of us are color-blind, and pretending that we are doesn't help anyone.

Oh, it's a nice sentiment. What we're trying to say, when we claim to be color-blind, is that we accept Dr. King's mandate to judge people by the content of their character, not the color of their skin. That we are not racist. That's good and right.

But the color-blind argument also dismisses the reality that people *do* have different experiences based on the color of their skin. These can be good experiences, like cultural traditions, or bad experiences, like discrimination, but they are very real and important to recognize. I mean, when I see my biracial cousins, I see my cousins, not a group of big black men. I could claim to be color-blind. But my supposed color blindness wouldn't change the fact that even in our little town, my cousins avoid stopping to help strangers for fear of frightening them. Ignoring that reality might make *me* feel better, but it wouldn't help my cousins. In fact, it could be dangerous for them.

The world is not color-blind, and pretending that it is only soothes the conscience of the dominant group. But if you shouldn't teach your children to ignore race, what *should* you teach them? Here are some ideas.

TALK ABOUT IT

Some people believe that talking about race will make your child notice differences they wouldn't otherwise. That's just not true. As my brother so masterfully demonstrated, kids notice. Yes, talking about race can be awkward, particularly since the Western world has such a shameful history in this area. But clamming up or acting horrified when your kid mentions race will only teach them that there is something very wrong or shameful in talking about it. Don't perpetuate the cycle.

DIVERSIFY

This is easier to accomplish in some parts of the world than others, but the more exposure your children have to people from different cultures, religions, and ethnicities, the better. People tend to fear what they don't understand, and love is the best antidote to fear. Same goes for you, mama. Be intentional about stretching your social circles.

BE A GOOD EXAMPLE

Cultivate an open heart and mind, and be willing to learn from people whose experiences and perspectives are different than yours. Disrupt the white ghetto on your bookshelf (it doesn't matter what ethnicity you are—most bookshelves are whitewashed) and read books written by people of color. Seek out friends and mentors of different races, and put yourself under their tutelage. Lay down your fear, your defensiveness, and your desire to look good, and engage with boldness and humility.

Yes, talking about race can be awkward, but not talking about it can be devastating. Let's embrace God's world in all its beautiful color and diversity, and teach our kids to do so as well.

Read a Book

"There are many little ways to enlarge your child's world.
Love of books is the best of all."

—Jacqueline Kennedy Onassis

When people ask where I grew up, I'm always tempted to say "Narnia." My family moved so often that there is no simple answer to that question, but C. S. Lewis's fantasy world was as familiar as my own backyard(s), and I probably spent more time there. Lewis wasn't my only literary love: I cleared dead plants out of *The Secret Garden* with Mary, Dickon, and Colin; explored hidden passageways with Nancy Drew; survived a shipwreck with *The Black Stallion*; and traveled the Oregon Trail countless times, with countless companions, in countless books.

Books were my life. But instead of detracting from my interactions with the real world, books deepened them. The insights, empathy, and new ideas I gleaned from reading were an integral part of my development.

I'm sure you know how important it is to read to your child. But there's more to life than Dr. Seuss, Little Golden Books, and paperbacks featuring their favorite TV characters. There are many wonderful books out there that can help your child develop mentally, emotionally, socially, and, yes, spiritually. I'm not just talking about Christian books, either. Christian books are wonderful, but I'd choose a great book with a noble theme over a mediocre one that wears its theology on its sleeve any day.

Personally, I think every family should check out the Sonlight homeschooling curriculum, whether they homeschool or not. It's chock full of incredible, age-appropriate books that will open your children's eyes to the beautiful, diverse bigness of the world, the gorgeous, all-encompassing bigger-ness of God, and how God calls people just like them to participate in his mission to save it. Seriously, Sonlight's book choices are incredible. Just make sure you set a budget before you get on their website; a book lover could go broke there!

Set a regular time to read with your family—a chapter during breakfast, after dinner, or before bed. Check out audiobooks from your local library, and listen to them together while you're doing chores, or driving to dance practice, or are on a family road trip. If your kids are reluctant readers, incentivize them with a special reward for reading a book you are sure they will enjoy, if they give it a chance. I offered my elementary schoolers cash to read *The Picture Bible* from cover to cover, and I am not even sorry. Best money I ever spent.

Reading can open whole new worlds to your child, and the best books can instill in them a passion to make a difference. So take your kids down to the local library, crack open a book, and see what a difference reading can make.

Babysit

Having teenagers is the best thing that ever happened to our family life. I know teenagers are supposed to be snotty and rebellious and all-around ornery, and mine have their moments. But I must have done something wrong, because all in all, my teens are absolute peaches. Or maybe I just feel that way about them because they can babysit when I need to be gone for a few hours.

Finding a good babysitter is *hard*. I've been blessed with some fabulous sitters over the years, but the problem with high school and college kids is that they grow up and get real jobs, and don't need to hang out with your little bundles of joy to afford their Abercrombie jeans anymore. Once, my family hit the jackpot—we lived a block from the small-town parsonage where the local pastor and his wife lived with their four teenagers. It was awesome. But finding and keeping good babysitters can be an incredible source of stress, especially if you don't have family nearby to help out in a pinch.

That's where you can come in, especially if you are home full time or part time. Being willing to babysit is an amazing blessing to parents who need a hand. Could you watch the neighbor boy for that awkward half hour between when his mom needs to leave for work and he has to get on the bus? Could you take those kids from church the one afternoon both parents have to work, so they don't have to fuss with daycare? Does your friend from the office really have to haul her toddlers along to her meeting with the divorce lawyer, or could they hang out at your place for a couple hours?

Single moms could use extra support in this area. I tell you what: my hats are off to these women. When I was a stay-at-home mom, I lived for the moment my husband walked through the door and there was someone else to help take care of the tinies. Knowing that help is not coming is hard to fathom. But this is where we moms can shoulder each other's burdens. Who are the single moms in your circles? (If you're a single mom yourself, this is still a good question to ask.) What do they need? A Saturday afternoon to themselves? Someone to watch their kids so grocery shopping isn't three hours of chaos? Backup childcare for when the baby is sick? How can you look out for one another?

For the record, I'm not just suggesting that stay-at-home moms should minister to single moms; actually, there's an amazing single mom at my house right now, taking care of some stuff I've been too sick to do while recovering from a nasty bout of pneumonia. (I just tottered out to get some coffee, and she ordered me back to bed and my laptop, like the good Jewish mother she is. "You have no business being out of bed. I can see it in your EYES!") She's the first friend I thought to S.O.S. when I knew I'd need help. And, boy, did she come through.

We all need friends like that. And often, those friends are made by offering to watch each other's kids—by being the childcare safety net they may not have otherwise. My husband has always said that the test of a true friend is whether you could call them for help if your car breaks down; I say the test of true family is whether you could call them to watch your kids. Can you be that person for someone in your community? The adopted auntie parents could call in a crisis, or kids could call in an emergency? The blessings go both ways, and the impact can be eternal.

Planting Seeds of Justice and Mercy

By Beth Bruno

I woke up to the reality of global poverty and injustice when my kids were seven, four, and one. As their mother, I took my power of indoctrination very seriously and began looking for ways to "kid-ify" all that I was learning. I had no idea that planting those early seeds of activism would transform our family.

When I read about the horrors of child labor in the cocoa industry, I packed up my preschoolers and visited nearby grocery stores with letters to the managers, urging them to consider the impact of slave labor in their supply chain. My kids each chose a Fair Trade chocolate bar to sample, and that Halloween, we gave out mini Fair Trade chocolates with an info card attached.

Upon learning how girls' education transforms communities in third-world countries, I urged the kids to go through their toys for a free garage sale. We filled our driveway with all the stuff and made posters that read, "Everything is free! Donations accepted for Pennies for Peace – Girls' Education in Afghanistan." They walked around with jars, collecting change for Afghan girls to go to school.

We started sponsoring a boy in Rwanda and giving small loans to women in the Middle East. I taped a world map next to our kitchen table and we prayed over these precious individuals we were helping in small ways.

As my kids grew, questions and curiosity turned into suggestions until, eventually, they were making their own plans. Without realizing it, I had planted seeds of mercy and justice that had taken root and begun to sprout.

Years after I dragged her to grocery stores, my youngest and I passed a number of homeless people camping on the capitol's lawn. She asked what they were doing, and a whole conversation ensued. A few weeks later, after I shared about my day doing art projects with homeless teens, she asked why they didn't have homes and where they showered. Then she said, "I think we are supposed to be the ones to take care of them." Gulp!

In an effort to appease her and respond, we made twenty bags of essentials to have ready when we passed homeless people. But it felt as if my daughter might be more attuned to God's heart than me.

Not long after, we learned of a program in which families provide homes for youth in transition. These are teens in chaos, without adult family members to live with, who need something immediate and temporary. Kids who might otherwise end up trafficked. We had a family meeting, and my husband and I were the only ones hesitating.

My son gave up his room for two months for our twenty-year-old guest. We were all sad when he left abruptly. My daughter gave up her room for a thirteen-year-old, whose pills I hid at night, along with the knives and scissors. They learned firsthand the effect of depression on teens.

As a family, we have changed. What began as my indoctrination and intentional shaping of their young hearts toward God's heart for justice has turned into mutual discipleship.

My little activists are challenging me every day to see the way God sees. I cannot wait to see who they become. When we open ourselves up to be used by God, the small things morph into bigger things, as he empowers us to do still more—children and adults alike.

Beth Bruno is the founder and director of A Face to Reframe, a nonprofit committed to preventing human trafficking in northern Colorado through arts, training, and community building. After spending ten years on staff with Cru, seven of which were in Turkey, she now writes about women in ministry, girls becoming women, and exploited women on her blog, bethbruno.org.

Because They Said So!

Bright Ideas from Mentor Moms

Help your kids see their school as their mission field. Every year before school, we take a walk around the school grounds the night before classes start and pray for the teachers, staff, and students at the school. We ask the kids about classmates who seem to be struggling and pray for them throughout the year and encourage them to show God's love to all of the kids. Our kids might be the only Jesus some of these students ever see.
—Nicole T. Walters, mama of two

Before Christmas, place a surprise on the doorknob of your neighbor's front door. Buy a dime-store red Christmas sock and stuff it with homemade cookies and merry wishes. Don't forget to sign the card!
—Margaret Philbrick, mama of three

Rent a bounce house! I'd tried to do elaborate and Pinterest-worthy cards and treats for Christmas; they were all half finished and undistributed come January. For Easter, I left a very simple printed flyer with each of the neighbors on our block, inviting them to enjoy a bounce house and simple barbecue (chicken apple sausages) and bring a treat to share with everyone. We do not live on a block where people talk to each other, but thirty people came, and many others emailed, thankful for the invitation. It was more fun than leaving something on their door, because we actually got to talk to everyone.
—Liz Ditty, mama of two

I try to model servanthood by holding doors for people, putting my shopping cart in the proper place, picking up trash when I see it on the ground, putting things in their proper place, and greeting people when they pass by. The little things you do daily can make a huge impact on your children and how they interact with the world.
—Lorie Lee, mama of one

It is now routine in our home that the last Friday of every month we will be making breakfast casseroles for the local homeless shelter. My son chops onions while my daughter cooks the sausage and I'm grating cheese. Cracking open a couple dozen eggs gets everyone laughing, as we regularly have to fish out bits of shells. The casseroles sit overnight, and I bake them early in the morning. Sometimes we all go to serve; other times we only drop off the casseroles.
—Sharon R. Hoover, mama of two

If you live in a big city, you see the homeless on street corners and at red lights. While I have stopped giving money to these individuals, I always have prepackaged food in my car to give away. It is not ideal to have a conversation at a red light, but every time I have given out food it has been well received. This is a great teachable moment for my child.
—Lorie Lee, mama of one

Your kids are not accessories to prove your worth as a mom or human being. They are people for you to love and instruments God will use to shape your character. Sometimes that's a really painful process, but it pushes us deeper into our need and to the radical love of the Father for his children.
—Ashley Hales, mama of four

POWER OUTLET SIX

Preach, Sister!

I've always been fascinated by Timothy, from the New Testament. We don't discuss him much in church, but when we do, he is typically portrayed as a timid young man with a nervous stomach, a clean-living mama's boy who basked in the warmth of Paul's fatherly affection. That may be true. But it is also true that Timothy was a towering figure in early Christianity who pioneered new mission fields, led tumultuous churches, co-wrote several of the Epistles, was imprisoned at least once, and, if tradition is correct, was martyred for disrupting a parade in honor of the goddess Diana. Not quite the mousy little man we portray him to be, huh? Timothy's outspoken mentor, Paul, attracts the spotlight, but Paul himself said that he had no one else like him—that our boy Timmy was the crème de la crème of Christian leaders, because he knew how to love.

I love Paul's advice to Timothy in 2 Timothy 1:6–7, and wish I could speak it over every woman in the church: "For this reason I remind you to fan into flame the gift of God, which is in you through the laying on of my hands. For the Spirit God gave us does not make us timid, but gives us power, love and self-discipline."

Sisters, we are not called to be timid. We are called to be powerful, loving, and self-disciplined.

Sometimes I feel like the church encourages women to be timid—that some equate cultivating a gentle and quiet spirit, much like that of Timothy or Jesus (who described himself as being gentle and humble in heart), with scurrying into the shadows like little church mice whenever anyone so much as looks at you. Nothing could be further from the truth. Gentleness is not opposed to strength—it is opposed to the abuse of power. Quietness is not opposed to the proclamation of truth—it is opposed to the chaos of thoughtless speech. Being a gentle soul who cherishes your mother's teaching, values relationships above accomplishments, and would just as soon let someone else run the show doesn't mean that God isn't calling you to lead. In fact, it may be exactly what qualifies you for the job. The world has enough brash, power-hungry control freaks clawing themselves into positions of influence. What we need are more gracious, humble servant-leaders who will put other people's needs before their own and lead with integrity, without losing sight of the fruits of the Spirit.

As followers of Jesus, each and every one of us has been called to ministry. Some of those callings may require more chutzpah than we think we possess; but, sisters, we are not called to be timid. We are not called to turn back when we hit obstacles, or duck behind the nearest man when the light and heat become hard to bear, or scurry into the shadows when someone looks at us askance. We are called to be powerful, loving, and self-disciplined. To soldier on with whatever task God has assigned to us, just like Timothy. Just like Christ. Just like so many faithful, courageous women and men who have gone before us.

You ready? Let's do this thing.

Tell Your Story

I used to volunteer with a para-church ministry that sent short-term mission teams all over the globe. We coached the team members on how to share their testimonies, but whenever we reached that part of the training, the people who had grown up in loving, stable Christian homes became quiet and insecure. They didn't have a dramatic conversion story, so they felt like they didn't have anything of significance to share. A few of them even confessed to wishing they had some sordid past, just so they had a "better" testimony.

That is messed up.

Sharing our testimony is one of the most effective ways of sharing our faith, but we have some weird ideas about what that means. Sure, it's impressive to hear a dynamic speaker share about how God plucked their lives out of the depths of an earthly hell, but as mesmerizing as those stories are, they're not incredibly relatable. Not for most of us, anyway. What we need to hear, and what our friends who don't know Jesus need to hear, is how God is working in the ordinariness of our daily lives. How does God's grand story of redemption intersect with your story?

Spend some time in thought and prayer, considering the ways in which walking with Jesus has affected your life. Did God carry you through that rough third year of marriage? Did your faith give you the courage you needed to go back to school, or quit your job, or pursue a new path in life? Are the Proverbs teaching you the value of having patience with your children? Did God's people come around you when your first child was born hundreds of miles away from your family?

While you're thinking through the stories that are the center-piece of your testimony—the things you would share at a MOPS group or church service—don't forget to think about what God is doing in your life right now. How is God shaping and challenging and changing you? Let's be honest—weaving those things into your everyday conversations will generally have a lot more impact than standing up in front of a group of church folks and pontificating on your past.

How is God's story intersecting with your story? That's your testimony. Be intentional about sharing it, whether you're standing in front of a congregation or sitting across from your cousin, whether you're on a mission trip to Sri Lanka or just trying to get out of the grocery store alive. You don't need a dramatic conversion story—just a little boldness, authenticity, and intentionality.

Tell God's Story

Quick: You're on a plane that's about to crash, and you have two minutes to explain the gospel to your seatmate. What do you say?

I know, I know. Those sorts of gimmicky fear tactics have a lot more to do with feature-length evangelistic films and earnest young youth pastors than they do with real life. But really. What is the gospel? How would you explain it to someone, clearly and concisely, without resorting to Sunday school jargon they are unlikely to understand? (I'm looking at you, "Jesus-in-my-heart." He's God of the universe, not a roundworm parasite.)

At this point, I am tempted to launch into a long, seminary-esque exposition on the Roman usage of the term "gospel" and its relationship to the kingdom of God, but that defeats the purpose of the whole clear-and-concise thing. Besides, N. T. Wright does a better job of that than I could, anyway. So instead, I'll expand on this simple explanation of the gospel thought up by my favorite practical theologian, my husband Aaron: God set it up, we messed it up, Jesus fixed it up, we've got to give it up.

GOD SET IT UP

God created everything that is, and he created human beings with the capacity to love him and live in relationship with him.

WE MESSED IT UP

But instead of living in a loving relationship with God, trusting that he was looking out for our best interests, we rebelled and made choices that hurt ourselves and others, and even God. The consequences of our wrong actions, and of other people's wrong actions against us, have led to brokenness of all kinds: broken relationships,

143

broken lives, broken bodies, broken hearts. Ultimately, the wrong actions lead to both spiritual and physical death.

JESUS FIXED IT UP
But God wasn't willing to abandon his beloved creation to destruction and despair. The moment sin entered the world, God began working to set things right again. Eventually, God entered the world in human form, in the person of Jesus. He showed us how human beings are supposed to live, and allowed himself to be put to death on a cross, accepting all the sin and suffering and brokenness the world could throw at him. But instead of being overcome by our sin, he overcame it. Instead of being conquered by death, he rose again on the third day, conquering it. He did all of this for us, to make it possible for us to be saved. Jesus is greater than our brokenness. Jesus is greater than our sin. Jesus is greater than death. And he wants to save us from all of it, if we will let him.

WE'VE GOT TO GIVE IT UP
But we've got to let him. God never has, and never will, force us into a relationship with him. That wouldn't be much of a relationship, would it? And it's a relationship God wants and is inviting us into. It's not just about agreeing with a certain set of beliefs or praying to ask God for forgiveness, although that is certainly part of it. It's about walking with God day in and day out, growing in our faith as we follow in Jesus' footsteps and allow our hearts to become more like his.

So, where are you at with all this? Are you ready to accept Jesus' offer of a fresh start in your relationship with God?

So there you have it, friends. The gospel in two minutes, maybe three. Of course, there are many different ways to explain it, and if you don't like how I did it, there are tons of evangelistic resources that you can draw on instead. But make sure you know God's story: the grand story of redemption we call the gospel or good news. Make sure you can explain it clearly and succinctly, keeping the Christian jargon to a minimum. And then tell it, tell it, tell it—to your children, to your friends, to everyone you meet.

Listen Up!

Several years ago, I went through the Evangelical Covenant Church's training to be an AVA (Advocacy for Victims of Abuse) advocate, who could walk alongside women living in, escaping from, or recovering from abusive relationships. The training was incredible, but what really stuck with me was what they said about the power of listening. The instructor warned us against getting frustrated when women talked about their traumatic experiences over and over but never seemed to take action to improve their situation. "Just listening is incredibly powerful," she said. "It gives them a safe space to process what happened, and begin to think about how they should respond."

She went on to explain that memories are stored in the limbic brain—the nonverbal, instinctual, and sometimes subconscious part of our brain that is responsible for our survival instincts and our emotions. When people have trauma floating around in there, they are likely to react to those memories in subconscious, instinctual, emotional ways. In order for healing to occur and positive action to take place, those memories need to be processed by the frontal lobe—the reasoning, planning, discerning part of our brain that gives us the ability to speak and write. And it turns out that using those powers of speech is the best way to transfer the custody of those memories from our instinctual brain to our logical one.

Talking it out really *is* the first step to healing and change. It's not touchy-feely psychobabble; it's brain science.

People with traumatic memories aren't the only ones who need a listening ear. How many times have you hashed out some issue with a friend, mentor, or coworker, and suddenly gained clarity on what you needed to do? Frontal lobe, baby. Talking kicks it into gear.

Do you get what this means? This means that one of the most powerful things you could ever do for a person is just listen to them. Give them your full attention, even when it's uncomfortable. Don't give in to the temptation to interrupt them with correction or advice—hear them out, and let them process. You'll get your opportunity to reply, if you must. Nod and ask clarifying questions so that they know you're really paying attention. Remember that when you're listening and they're talking, the focus should be on their thoughts and feelings and needs, not yours. Put yours aside to ponder later. Cultivate what clergy refer to as a "non-anxious presence"—we want our friends to freak out when we tell them about the amazing deal we got on our new boots, but not when we're spilling our guts about our creepy uncle, or our husband's layoff, or our mom's cancer diagnosis.

The ministry of listening can be far more powerful, and far more difficult, than most of us ever imagined. As heavy as some people's stories can be, it's an amazing privilege to be invited into their inner world, to help them process and bear those burdens. Respect that trust, and learn to listen well.

Don't Just Talk about Jesus— Live Like Jesus

By Marlena Graves

A few years ago, something occurred to me that is in all probability glaringly obvious to anyone reading these words. It is this: we can talk about God a lot, darken the doors of our churches whenever they are open, read the Bible every day, know the Scriptures, and even have a degree in theology—all without living like Jesus. We can engage in lots of God talk and still live godless lives. The thing is, we seldom realize what we're doing. We can subtly confuse our talking about Jesus and studying the Word with actually living like Jesus.

I started thinking about all of this during the five years I was a resident director on a Christian university campus. We had Bible studies galore and chapel five days a week. Each week, students were required to engage in some sort of Christian activity like a ministry or Bible study outside of Sunday mornings.

But it kept occurring to me that if the young women in my dorm could not love their roommates and hall mates who were their closest neighbors, did it really matter that they studied the Bible all of the time or went on missions trips every summer? As James said, we must be doers of the Word and not just hearers (or studiers!) of the Word; otherwise we are deceiving ourselves (James 1:22). In my day-in and day-out interactions with faculty, staff, and students, and in knowing myself, I saw that it was incredibly easy for us to fool ourselves into thinking we were living like Jesus

because we were reading and studying the Bible, hearing sermons in chapel, and talking about him all of the time.

So I challenged the students in my dorm to love their actual neighbors, their closest neighbors, who turned out to be their roommates and hall mates.

I no longer live on campus or even in the same town, but the lesson of loving my actual and closest neighbors, instead of just talking about loving them, has stuck with me. Now I am on the pastoral care team at my church as the minister of pastoral care. I talk and pray with people nearly every single day. It would be ludicrous, and ultimately damaging, for me to talk, pray, and sermonize about loving God and my neighbors without concretely loving God and my actual neighbors!

I often think about the ridiculousness of pulling out of my driveway and failing to know and love my actual neighbors while passing them by on my way to church. Moreover, I'd be a rock star hypocrite if I ignored or dismissed the needs of my family members (my closest neighbors) on my way to minister to others.

I think the true measure of our faith and ministry is how we love those closest to us. How do we love the neighbors who irritate us? How do we love those across the street, down the road, or beside us? How do we love those in our churches and our local communities?

Marlena Graves (MDiv) is the author of A Beautiful Disaster: Finding Hope in the Midst of Brokenness *(Brazos Press 2014). Hearts & Minds bookstore awarded it the Best Book on Spiritual Formation by a First Time Writer (2014). Marlena is also a bylined writer for* Christianity Today, Our Daily Journey (Our Daily Bread), *and other venues, and is on staff at her church.*

Preach at a Women's Correctional Facility

"I've been preaching to a captive audience. Literally."

It was the first night of my church's annual family camp, and a bunch of us were sitting around the campfire, singing worship songs and sharing testimonies. There was the normal fare—a verse that had spoken to someone that morning, a prodigal returned home—but I about fell off the bench when Jenni, a vivacious home-schooling mom, shared that she was preaching regularly at the local jail.

Evidently Jenni's father was active in Prison Fellowship ministries. They had been planning an Easter service for the inmates but hit a snag. Men weren't allowed to go into the women's section, and since all the pastors involved were male, there was no one to speak to the women. So the male inmates would get the Easter hymns, the hope-filled Scriptures, and the message of Christ's victory over sin and death, while the women, first to observe the risen Christ, would languish in their cells.

This was *not* okay with Jenni. As soon as she heard about the predicament, she pulled out her Bible, prepared her message, and shared God's Word with the women. Not just on Easter, but on many, many Sundays after that.

I am aware that the idea of preaching to anyone, much less a crowd of inmates, is intimidating to most middle-class moms. Public speaking tops the list of common fears, and many of us consciously or subconsciously consider preaching the domain of men. But some of you have a gift for speaking, teaching, and preaching, whether you've acknowledged and developed it or not. And the gifts God gives are meant to be used for good, not hidden away under layers of unchecked insecurity and manufactured modesty.

Remember 2 Timothy 1:6–7? "For this reason I remind you to fan into flame the gift of God, which is in you through the laying on of my hands. For the Spirit God gave us does not make us timid, but gives us power, love and self-discipline." Don't hide your light under a laundry basket. Fan it into flame, and let it shine!

Many people find God when they are incarcerated, but women make up such a tiny percentage of the prison population that few ministries focus on them. That's a tragedy, because female inmates are much more likely than their male counterparts to suffer from a host of maladies and injustices. Information from the National Institute of Corrections and the U.S. Bureau of Justice Statistics paints a bleak picture. The average female inmate is a mother in her early to mid-thirties.[1] She was locked up on a property or drug-related offense, and has never committed a violent crime.[2] She is a long-term abuse survivor who suffers from chronic illness and mental health issues,[3] and she is twice as likely as male prisoners to attempt suicide.[4]

These precious women have been drinking a deadly cocktail of poverty, neglect, abuse, and addiction since they were old enough to hold a sippy cup, and they're unwittingly passing it on to their kids. They desperately need the living water only Christ can provide. Are you willing to step out of your comfort zone to offer it to them?

Do some research. Who is reaching out to female inmates in your area? Would the women benefit from a Bible study or a MOPS group? Do they have a chance to worship together and hear solid teaching to encourage them in their walk with God? Or has their gender effectively cut them off from corporate worship? If so, what might God be calling you to do about it?

"I needed clothes and you clothed me, I was sick and you looked after me, I was in prison and you came to visit me" (Matt. 25:36).

Gather a Group

Ministry requires two things: God and people. Hopefully you allow God to minister to you, and I am certain that you minister to the people you interact with on a daily basis. But if you want to broaden that ministry and make it more intentional, one of the best things you can do is start a group.

Perhaps you'd like to host a small group at your home or start a Bible study that meets at your favorite café once a week. Great! But your group doesn't necessarily have to be teaching-oriented to be an effective ministry. Groups of all kinds can be a blessing to the members and the people they serve.

Book clubs are a great way to interact and facilitate conversations around tough topics. You can use Christian books if you want, but you may get more traction discussing books that are all the buzz right now. Talking about the underlying philosophies of the book, the ethics at play, and the issues the characters struggle with can be incredibly meaningful. Meeting once a month is doable for most people, and it's frequent enough that they can come to know and trust the other members.

Maybe art is your thing. I have a friend who invites people to her church two evenings per month to work on any art or craft projects they have going. If they aren't particularly artistic, she helps them come up with ideas and supplies. But for the most part, it is just an opportunity for women to come together, create in community, and talk about whatever is on their hearts and minds.

Are you a cancer warrior, an abuse survivor, or the parent of a child with special needs? Look into what it would take for you to start a support group, bringing together others who have struggled

down the same path. Lots of ministry and mutual encouragement can happen there.

Maybe you want to get a group of people together to serve at the soup kitchen, or pick up litter on the side of the highway, or perform random acts of kindness one Saturday per month. Do it! Few things pull people together as well as working toward a common goal, in service to God and others.

Starting a group doesn't have to be a big deal. Just gather a group of people, discuss what you would like to do, and give it a try. Keep it low key at first, and grow into it. Who knows what God will do in and through your group?

Get Educated about Other Religions

The best part of growing up as a missionary kid was the exposure I had to other cultures and religions. I attended school with Muslims and Buddhists. I lived next door to Jains and people who practiced African traditional religions. They were my friends and neighbors: the people who carpooled me to school, cooked me tasty food, recruited me to babysit their daughters, and opportunistically gifted me their grown children's three-foot-tall stuffed animals (which impressed me much more than my parents). I learned about their religious beliefs because they were part of my life, and also because I wanted to share Jesus with them.

It was just a given, in the missionary community I grew up in, that if you wanted to share Jesus with someone, you should understand where they were coming from. What do they already believe? How are their beliefs similar to yours, and how are they different? What writings do they hold to be sacred, and what do those writings say? Who do they believe Jesus was? Learning about different religions not only helped missionaries minister more effectively—building on points of connection while avoiding ignorant mistakes and unnecessary offense—it demonstrated honor, respect, and a willingness to have an open dialogue, instead of sticking our fingers in our ears and monologuing about Christianity.

When we moved back to the States, though, things were different. Many of my parents' evangelical friends were concerned that I had so many friends who weren't Christians and that I actively studied their religions. Luckily, my parents just rolled their eyes and pointed me toward books and resources they thought would be helpful. But I often wonder how many Christians feel like my

parents' friends—afraid to learn about other religions, or acknowledge anything good in them, for fear it could sway their faith.

But we are not called to live in fear. We are called to be deeply rooted and built up in Christ, strengthened in the faith. Then, we are called to go out like sheep among wolves and engage the world, being as shrewd as serpents and as innocent as doves.

Hey, it was Jesus' idea, not mine.

If you feel called to share Jesus with people who adhere to a different religion, whether it's your Wiccan friend from school, the community of Muslim immigrants across town, or the mission field of Hindu-dominated India, study up on what they believe. Look for good sources—instead of reading inflammatory best sellers that "expose the evil secrets of (insert religion)," search out books by missionaries who have dedicated their lives to that community. Ask your friends questions, and then listen to what they have to say, without trying to correct their theology, defend your beliefs, or shut them down. Asking questions is a great way to open up conversations about religious issues, and they may be thrilled to share with you.

If your friends ask you questions you don't know the answers to, or challenge your faith in ways that make you feel uncomfortable, allow that to drive you deeper into God's Word as you seek understanding. In my experience, evangelism is the best thing you can do to further your own spiritual growth. If you are up for a challenge, pray, put on the full armor of God, and read their religious texts. When we lived in Liberia, my father would read the Koran, our friend Mohammed would read the Bible, and they would get together regularly to discuss what they were learning. My father gained a better understanding of Islam, and Mohammed gained a relationship with Christ.

Don't be afraid to learn about other religions. It's an important part of reaching the world for Jesus. Root yourself in Christ. Dig deep into the Bible. And then, get out there and engage.

Become an Insufferable Know-It-All

Pastors get it all the time. Someone comes swirling into their office, practically vibrating with emotion, and starts expounding on what the church *should* be doing. The church *should* be reaching out to the homeless in the city center. They *should* be filling baby bottles with money for the local crisis pregnancy center. They *should* start an Awana program, or do something about human trafficking in India, or visit the local nursing homes, or do a collection drive for the food pantry.

Those are all great ideas, but there's a problem. Your pastor is only one person. One *really busy* person, in most cases. If they're smart, they'll say something along the lines of "Wow, I can see that you're really passionate about this. Have you considered whether God may be calling *you* to do something about it?"

Yeah, they're passing the buck. But only after you tried to pass it to them. And besides, they're probably right. If God is stirring your heart on some issue, it's probably not to convince you to go talk to your pastor. It's probably to convince you to engage the issue yourself.

What are you passionate about? If you're not sure, ask yourself, what breaks your heart? What makes you angry? What fills you with joy, and peace, and purpose? For some people, it is orphan care or human trafficking. Some people are concerned about good theology and careful teaching. Some people have a heart for children's ministry, or are infuriated that only men are serving communion, or are passionate about racial reconciliation, or are concerned about neighbors struggling with mental illness and addiction. If God has laid it on your heart, maybe it's because you're supposed to do something about it.

"But Jenny," you may be saying, "I have three kids under the age of five. I can barely manage a trip to the grocery store, much less head up some big initiative on homelessness or human trafficking or mental health issues. That's why I bought this book in the first place. Because I want to help, but I don't have the bandwidth."

That's fine. Unless you hear some booming voice from heaven, urging you to take action, it's a good idea to pace yourself. But do you know what you can do when your kids are tiny? You can learn about the issues that are close to your heart. You can read books, and sign up for newsletters, and participate in online discussion groups, and grow in wisdom. You can become something of an expert, and share that expertise with others.

So, say your passion is rescuing girls from human trafficking. You're probably not going to fly over to Cambodia and participate in brothel raids (at least not until the baby is weaned), but you can head down to the library and check out books on the topic. You can get online and learn the signs that indicate someone may be a trafficking victim, and what you should do if you suspect that they are. You can watch documentaries on human trafficking; connect with anti-trafficking groups in your community or online; and keep your eyes open at fruit stands, and in nail salons, and at hotels. And most of all, you can share this information with everyone in your circle of influence, raising their awareness, giving them the information they need if they ever come across that issue, and perhaps igniting a passion in their heart as well.

Who knows? Your passion might even convince your pastor that the church should do something about it.

Get Comfortable with Being Uncomfortable

The first time I was asked to preach was one of the most terrifying experiences of my life. My church was going through a series on the benefits of marriage (as opposed to living together), and my pastor, who had been mentoring me through a ministry degree, asked me to preach on the impact those issues had on women. I was thrilled and honored and flat-out terrified.

See, women didn't preach at our church. Oh, a female missionary would come through and share a message every couple years, and once the executive minister of women's ministries for the Evangelical Covenant Church traveled to our area and gave the sermon. But in general? Women didn't even pass the offering plates or serve communion. I would be the exception to a long-standing, though unofficial, rule. And I wasn't going to be hopping on a plane and skipping town once it was over. I had to continue living in that community.

So I went over my sermon again and again. I freaked out about my wardrobe choices (what *do* women wear to preach in, anyway?) and scoured thrift stores for something formal enough that I wouldn't look girly and feminine enough to make it clear I wasn't trying to look masculine. I did a whole lot of praying and wrestling with God about my fears, and I rehearsed possible scenarios in my mind. How would I respond if some people walked out when I got up to speak? What would I do if someone stood up and started yelling at me? I got really, really uncomfortable. And I did it anyway.

It turned out to be one of the best things that I ever did. The Holy Spirit moved, people were blessed, and within a couple years

of that first terrifying experience, I was enrolled in an MDiv program and preaching regularly as a member of pastoral staff.

Now, some of you may be uncomfortable with this story, or with the idea of a woman preaching or pastoring. That's okay. To be honest, I was as well, although I didn't have any biblical or theological qualms about it. I had just never seen it done. But none of that is really the point. The point is, the longer I walk with Christ, the more convinced I become that God does not call us to be comfortable.

Where did we get this idea that life with Christ is supposed to be a cozy, conservative, risk-averse parody of a Hallmark Channel Christmas special anyway? That's certainly not how it happened in the Bible. No, God consistently challenged his people, calling them out into the unknown, calling them past their own limits, calling them beyond the bounds of their culture and earthly allegiances, beyond the bounds of physics sometimes, into a new place where they would be completely reliant on him. Out of Ur. Into the wilderness. Onto the waves.

This issue is amplified for leaders. Leaders are, by definition, blazing new trails, or leading people further along a certain path. It's a sobering responsibility, and if you're not at least a little bit terrified, you probably should be. God save us from the arrogance that makes us charge blindly ahead, and the apathy that prevents us from leading people down difficult but necessary paths!

We need to get comfortable with being uncomfortable. That queasy, terrified feeling in the pit of your stomach when you've stepped outside your comfort zone doesn't mean you've stepped outside God's will (although if you have doubts about that, it's really important to pray; search the Scriptures; and get wise, godly counsel). It may mean that you are walking straight into the center of it.

Because They Said So!

Bright Ideas from Mentor Moms

Read the local newspaper (or the local newspaper online). It sounds so easy, or maybe archaic, but it's the first step to really understanding and then engaging the struggles and success stories just outside your door. What are people proud of? What do they need? Who's already engaged in the work of restoration? Then comes the outreach and evangelism: where can you fit in?
—Erin F. Wasinger, mama of three

*Get to know the immigrants in your community. Did you know that fewer than one in ten new arrivals to the United States will **ever** enter the home of an American-born citizen? There is a huge opportunity for cross-cultural ministry here, without buying a plane ticket or suffering jet lag! And the friendship (and food!) you'll share will be a blessing.*
—Catherine McNiel, mama of three

A great way for families to engage the global community is to engage refugees in your own backyard. I recently went through World Relief's volunteer training and became a Friendship Partner. I have been partnered with a family from Burma. I take them to the grocery store, explain banking, take their one-year-old to the park, and help them with their English. It is bumpy and not perfect, but it is engagement.
—Shayne Moore, mama of three

We have soup night every Tuesday in our homes in our neighborhood. Three or four homes are open with soup and an open table to any neighbors or anyone who needs a place at the table. It runs from October to March.
—Sheli Massie, mama of five

For years, my husband and I have used our spare bedroom as a "Jesus room," where we welcome Jesus in the form of people who need a free place to live for a few weeks or months. Guests have included a young social worker who used the saved rent to pay off school debt, a work colleague who needed to save up money to bring her kids to live with her, a woman who lost her job and was temporarily homeless, a college student who couldn't afford a dorm room, a summer White House intern, a former nun with early dementia—the list goes on. Such a blessing to us and to them, and a good example to our kids.

—Carolyn Parr, mama of three

Help your kids work through interpersonal conflicts in a way that is honoring to everyone involved. Keep a level head when your child tells you about problems they are having with other people—if you fly off the handle, or get defensive, or act ashamed, or start grumbling threats, they will think that is the appropriate way to respond to conflict. Don't excuse negative behaviors or bullying, but do help your kids think through what might be going on under the surface (whether they are on the giving or receiving end of the behavior), particularly if it involves other children. Teach your children about good boundaries, and be calm, compassionate, and firm.

—Jenny Rae Armstrong, mama of four

My mom makes extra food on Sundays and delivers it to the elderly in our neighborhood. I love this and have incorporated this into my life by making extra food and sharing it with people in my life.

—Lorie Lee, mama of one

Notes

[1] E. Ann Carson, *Prisoners in 2013*, Bureau of Justice Statistics of the U.S. Department of Justice, September 2014, www.bjs.gov/content/pub/pdf/p13.pdf.

[2] "Incarcerated Women," *Women's Health,* http://mchb.hrsa.gov/whusa12/pc /pages/iw.html (accessed October 19, 2015).

[3] Stephen J. Tripodi and Carrie Pettus-Davis, "Histories of Childhood Victimization and Subsequent Mental Health Problems, Substance Use, and Sexual Victimization for a Sample of Incarcerated Women in the US," www .ncbi.nlm.nih.gov/pmc/articles/PMC3547639 (accessed October 19, 2015).

[4] Christine Tartaro and David Lester, *Suicide and Self-Harm in Prisons and Jails* (Lanham, MD: Lexington Books, 2009), 55–56.

POWER OUTLET SEVEN

Go Girl! Empowering Women around the World

> "More girls were killed in the last 50 years, precisely because they were girls, than men killed in all the wars in the 20th century. More girls are killed in this routine gendercide in any one decade than people were slaughtered in all the genocides of the 20th century."
>
> —Nicholas D. Kristof, *Half the Sky: Turning Oppression into Opportunity for Women Worldwide*

The numbers are staggering. While women in the West have made great strides, millions of females around the world are routinely aborted, neglected, abused, sold into early marriage or slavery, and denied basic human rights. Some people cringe at terms like "feminism" or "women's rights," associating them with social changes they do not like. But oh, sisters. Aren't you glad that our great-grandmothers won us the right to vote our consciences? Aren't you glad that we have the right to pursue education, and own property, and have a job that pays fairly, whether we avail ourselves of those options or not? Aren't you glad that it is illegal for our parents to sell us into marriage or for our husbands to beat us, and that it *is* legal for us to drive a car and appear in public without a burka?

We have opportunities that women around the world are literally dying for. All that time we spend arguing about feminism and womanhood and whether it is better to stay home or take a job would be better spent fighting for women and girls suffering horrific injustices, simply because they are female.

If we're honest, though, things aren't always so hot here at home, either. One in four American women will fall victim to domestic violence at some point in her lifetime. One in seven will experience an attempted or completed rape. And while it's difficult to get hard and fast numbers on this last statistic, roughly one quarter of American women say they were sexually molested before their fourteenth birthday.[1] Societal oppression and violence against women pose a significant danger, not just to women, but to society as a whole.

Allow me to get theological for a moment. The devil has it in for women. Genesis 3:15 says "And I will put enmity between you and the woman, and between your offspring and hers; he will crush your head, and you will strike his heel." Yeah, Satan's not particularly fond of men either, but it was a woman, empowered by the Holy Spirit, who brought the Messiah (and Satan's ultimate destruction) into the world. Is it any surprise that Satan seems so intent to steal from, kill, and destroy women, and that so many crimes against women are sexual in nature?

Utterly predictable, and utterly despicable.

But there's good news. Jesus came to redeem and restore women, and we get to participate in his work. Plus, all the studies show that our efforts to empower women are making a difference! When women are educated and empowered, their lives, their children's lives, and their entire communities begin to change for the better. That's not surprising, since happy, healthy, educated mothers tend to raise happy, healthy, educated kids.

This section will give you ideas on how to help your suffering sisters, around the world and right here at home. Let's lock arms, raise the Jesus flag high, and march toward freedom!

Get Educated about Girl's Education

What if there were a silver bullet—one simple, all-encompassing way to address the cycle of extreme poverty, child mortality, the AIDS epidemic, and the orphan crisis in sub-Saharan Africa? What if I told you that it was as simple as sending girls to school?

It's true. Sending girls to school doesn't just prepare girls for their future; it protects their future by safeguarding them from a variety of social problems. Check out the following statistics.

EXTREME POVERTY

Every year of school that a girl attends up to eighth grade increases her earning potential by 10 to 20 percent. Every year of high school adds 15 to 20 percent to her eventual wages. And since women reinvest 90 percent of their income back into the health, education, and well-being of their families, compared to the 30 to 40 percent men reinvest, it is often the woman's contribution that breaks the cycle of extreme poverty and secures a better future for her children.[2] Go mama go!

OH, BABY!

Complications of pregnancy and childbirth are the leading cause of death for girls between the ages of fifteen and nineteen, and infants born to teen moms are 50 percent less likely to survive.[3] But the longer a girl stays in school, the more likely she is to put off childbearing until adulthood.

Statistically speaking, when a girl has at least seven years of education, she marries four years later and has 2.2 fewer children.[4] That makes a big difference for women struggling to raise healthy, well-nourished, educated kids. And of course, the more education the mother has, the healthier her children tend to be. Preparing food safely, watching for developmental markers—there is a big difference between what an illiterate fourteen-year-old does when her baby gets sick, and what a twenty-four-year-old with a college degree does. Educated mamas raise healthy kids.

HIV, AIDS, AND EDUCATION

The majority of people dying of AIDS in sub-Saharan Africa are young mothers in their twenties and thirties. Their early deaths are largely due to early marriage: teenage girls are partnered off with older men out of economic necessity. Abstinence education doesn't help a girl who has to marry to survive, and teaching girls about condoms only helps if she can convince her partner to use them every time (which is highly unlikely). But do you know what does help? School. In sub-Saharan Africa, female high school students are *five times less likely* to be infected with HIV than their out-of-school peers.[5] Think about what that means—not only for them, but for any children they eventually have.

ORPHAN CARE

Orphan care has become trendy in evangelicalism, and I am so glad that Christians are taking initiative in this area. But hear this. The best way to care for orphans is to care for their mamas, so they don't become orphans in the first place. Too many young mothers are dying in childbirth, from AIDS, or from diseases modern medicine could easily prevent or cure. Too many desperate mothers are turning their children over to orphanages because they can't keep them fed, much less healthy and educated. We like kid-focused causes because babies are cute and innocent and helpless, but what children need more than anything (aside from Jesus) are their mommies.

167

There is a reason the Bible pairs the support of the fatherless with support of the widows. The best way to help children is to empower their mamas. And the best way to empower their mamas is to give them the chance at an education.

How Maxi Pads Could Save the World

Remember when you got your first period? I'm sure we've all read those horror stories about girls who thought they were dying, or were too humiliated to tell anyone what was going on, but I was thrilled. I couldn't wait to get on the phone and tell my BFFs what had happened.

But my excitement waned after a few months. Is it just me, or are periods worse when you're in your teens? The cramping was intense, my flow was inconsistent, and it took a long time for my body to settle into a cycle I could track on a calendar. The pads in the early 1990s were not what they are today, and I felt insecure about using tampons. Like most middle schoolers, I was terrified that my period might catch me unawares, or a pad might leak through, and I would be humiliated in front of my classmates.

Now imagine being a twelve-year-old girl in the developing world, trying to manage your period by wadding old rags or plant leaves into panties you may or may not have, while attending a school with no running water or indoor plumbing.

You can see how this would be a problem.

Around the world, thousands of teenage girls miss school every month because they have no effective way to manage their periods. This puts them at a significant academic disadvantage, and many quit school entirely. This is a tragedy not just for the girls, but for everyone, since educating women is one of the most effective ways to lower poverty, safeguard public heath, and improve outcomes in their communities.

Luckily, many great organizations have sprung up to address this problem. AFRIpads manufactures reusable pads right in Uganda, employing local women. Days for Girls chapters assemble kits containing panties, pads, waterproof bags, and everything a girl needs to manage her period for up to three years. Students at the Art Center College of Design in California have invented an ingenious, inexpensive pod that allows girls to wash and dry their pads discreetly. Girls helping girls!

However, since menstruation has traditionally not been considered a polite topic of conversation, these organizations are only beginning to get traction. Every day of school these girls miss is a blow to their future and to ours. We need to act now.

There are many ways you can help. Consider organizing a period party at work or church to raise money for organizations that provide menstrual health kits. (I will leave the details up to Pinterest and your own imagination.) Check if there is a Days for Girls chapter in your area, or consider starting one. Buy your own feminine hygiene products from companies that give back; for instance, THINX donates seven AFRIpads for every pair of period panties they sell.

Menstruation is a normal, healthy part of female life, and no girl should be held back because she doesn't have the resources to manage her period. Let's unite, mamas, and get these girls back in school!

Get the Facts on Domestic Abuse

We always tell women to take precautions when they are out alone at night: to stay alert, walk with confidence, and keep to well-lighted areas. The truth of the matter is, though, women are much more likely to experience violence in their own homes than they are on the street.

Domestic violence is a huge problem. According to the Center for Disease Control's National Intimate Partner and Sexual Violence Survey, about one in three American women has experienced some form of domestic violence in her lifetime. One in four has experienced severe violence, such as being punched or slammed against a wall; one in ten has been raped; and nearly half of all women *and* men have experienced psychological aggression from an intimate partner. Almost 6 percent of women have experienced violence, rape, or stalking within the past year, and women between the ages of eighteen and thirty-four are most at risk.[6]

While it's tempting to think that domestic violence is a problem "out there," something that happens to alcoholics, dropouts, and women who wear too much eyeliner, the statistics don't change much among churchgoers. In fact, while men who attend church every week are among the least likely to abuse their wives, men who attend church occasionally are more likely to be abusive than non-churchgoers.[7]

Our natural reaction to statistics like this is to clutch our pearls, to weep and wail and gnash our teeth. That's an important part of addressing this issue, because righteous anger can stir us to righteous action. But abuse victims don't need our anger; they need shrewd, strategic support. So if a friend confides that she is being abused, or you sense that she is dropping hints, trying to tell you something without saying it outright, don't freak out. Take a few deep breaths, listen closely to what she has to say, and then help her think through what she needs to do to stay safe. The next Bright Idea will help you put together a safety plan.

Another reaction to statistics on domestic violence may be to dismiss or deny them, either because they are so far removed from your life experience that you can't believe they're true, or because they hit too close to home. It is extremely difficult for many people to admit that what they have been experiencing is abuse. It feels safer to believe that we were at least partially at fault for abusive incidents than to admit we were at the mercy of someone capable of overpowering us. That is terrifying. But oh, sisters. We have to look this issue in the eye. Denial may seem safer and easier than facing the truth, but it is the truth that will set us free.

God hates domestic violence. Malachi 2:16 (ironically the very passage that is often used to encourage women to stay in violent marriages) explains that God hates divorce *because* it was a form of violence men were committing against women who relied on them for protection. And in Matthew 19:8, Jesus explained that while divorce wasn't part of God's intent at creation, Moses had allowed it because men's hearts were hard. Why? To afford women some form of protection in a bad situation. Yes, divorce is a tragedy, and it's far from God's ideal. But so is abuse. So is violence. So is women and children living in fear because the man who should protect them terrorizes them.

God hates violence against women, and as his followers, we should too. The status quo is not acceptable. Let's keep our eyes open, and take thoughtful, prayerful action against abuse and for healthy, God-honoring relationships.

Make a Safety Plan

Statistics about domestic violence can be overwhelming. It's a huge problem, and it's hard to know where to begin to address it. I would suggest starting by learning how to make a safety plan. If you live in an unsafe situation, making a safety plan is one of the best things you can do for yourself and your children. If you are safe, helping a friend create a safety plan could be a great help.

KNOW THE NUMBERS

Of course you should call 911 in an emergency, but the trained advocates on the National Domestic Violence Hotline can help you anytime and get you connected with people and agencies in your area that can help you stay safe. Their number is 1-800-799-7233. Hearing-impaired folks can call 1-800-787-3224. Memorize the numbers you need. If you are not a victim of abuse, program the hotline's number into your phone. You never know when you will be with someone who needs that information.

BE CAUTIOUS ABOUT TECHNOLOGY

If you are researching safety plans or making a plan to escape, think twice about doing it on your home computer, where someone could access the browser history. Use a computer at a library, a friend's house, or a safe office environment. Also bear in mind that some phones, tablets, and even cars track your location through GPS and can be traced. Take the necessary precautions.

WHERE'S YOUR SAFE PLACE?

Some rooms in your house may be safer than others. If possible, try to stay near an exit, and away from rooms containing weapons, knives (don't run into the kitchen), or other dangerous objects.

PLAN YOUR ESCAPE ROUTE

In school, they teach kids that everyone should have a fire escape plan. You should also have an escape plan in case your partner becomes violent. How are you going to get out of the house, and where are you going to go? Do you know the route to a local emergency room or other safe place? How are your kids going to get out, and where should they go if you are not with them? Consider going over this emergency plan with your kids.

BACK IN

Back into your driveway and garage when you park, so you can drive away as quickly and safely as possible. Consider leaving the driver's side unlocked so you don't have to fumble for keys, but lock all the other doors.

PACK A BAG

It might be wise to have a bag of important items packed in case you need to leave home in a hurry, temporarily or otherwise. Consider leaving it with a trusted friend or at a church that is willing to help. A change of clothes is helpful, but you'll want to make sure you have some money, extra keys, copies of important documents such as birth certificates and green cards, banking information, and enough medication to last a couple days. Have a list of contact numbers in case you have to leave your phone behind, and don't forget to pack enough diapers, formula, and medicine to hold your kids over until you reach safety.

Champion Maternal Health

Home births have become all the rage. When my oldest was born, only the most crunchy-granola moms considered going through labor and delivery at home, but now, it's almost a badge of honor. That's fine, and I am thankful that women in the Western world can (for the most part) choose the birth experience that is going to make them the most comfortable, whether that is laboring in a pool in their living room or getting an epidural under the supervision of a full medical team. But "choose" is the key word here. Millions of mamas around the world don't have the healthcare options we in the West take for granted, or even look down our noses at.

Here are a couple statistics from the World Health Organization and Save the Children's 2014 State of the World's Mothers report:[8]

- Only 47 percent of women in poor countries have a doctor, nurse, or midwife present during delivery.
- Every day, approximately 800 women die from complications of pregnancy and childbirth that are completely preventable. Of those deaths, 99 percent happen in the developing world.
- Complications of pregnancy and childbirth are the leading cause of death for girls between the ages of fifteen and nineteen. Did you catch that? The leading cause of death. These girls are twice as likely to die as women who give birth in their twenties, and their babies are 50 percent less likely to survive. Girls giving birth at fourteen or younger are five times more likely to die than women in their twenties.
- There is a 1 in 3,700 chance that a woman in the developed world will die from pregnancy-related causes. There is a 1

in 120 chance that a woman in the developing world will die from pregnancy-related causes.

This is unacceptable.

But it's not all bad news! As of 2013, maternal mortality rates were 50 percent lower than they were in 1990. Our efforts are making a difference! But there is still so much more that needs to be done.

Of course what these mamas need more than anything is access to a strong healthcare system, and an end to military conflicts that damage the existing healthcare infrastructure. Childbirth is a surprisingly political issue. Here's a startling piece of trivia: During World War I, more American women died in childbirth than American men died on the battlefield. But once women got the vote and pushed through a piece of legislation to improve women's access to healthcare during pregnancy and childbirth, maternal and infant mortality rates plummeted.[9] As a Western woman, you have more political influence than you realize. Advocate for good maternal healthcare, in your nation and around the world, and don't let the politicos push it onto the back burner!

Clean birth kits are a stopgap measure for women giving birth in difficult circumstances. Soap, string, gauze, a fresh razor blade, plastic gloves, and a small plastic sheet drastically reduce the risk of infection during delivery. Make a donation to one of the many nonprofits that provide clean birth kits, or do a little research, gather your girlfriends, assemble a bunch of kits, and send them to a global distribution site. This would be an amazing activity to do at a baby shower. Pray for the people who will be using them as you make them—for the mama, the person attending the labor, and the baby who will be making his or her way into the world.

Mamas matter. Let's join hands and make sure that all mamas can have a safe, healthy pregnancy and delivery.

Stop Hating on Girls

You know what drives me nuts? When women who find out I have four sons compliment my luck, and then proceed to whine and moan about how moody and dramatic females are, like they need to prove their own point. My thoughts at such times are distinctly unfeminine, at least according to their standards. Sweet baby Jamison, hold your mama back!

Growing up on the mission field, I was taught that it is wrong to generalize. That making blanket statements about certain segments of the population is rude, damaging, and dehumanizing. That people begin to believe what is said about them if they hear it often enough, so generalizations not only dismiss people's potential, but actually limit it. My parents repeated this lesson so often that "Jenny, Don't Generalize" could have been my proper name.

So when women talk trash about their gender as a whole, I see a very, very dark shade of pink. Especially if their strong, lovely daughters happen to be standing right there, absorbing their mother's words about how emotionally volatile they are.

Have a little self-respect, ladies! And if that is too much to ask, at least quit throwing your daughters under the bus.

Allow me a short rant. With the possible exception of my nine-year-old, I am the least emotional person in my household. Granted, that's not saying much since we're all a bunch of angsty artists, and three of us are currently in varying stages of puberty. But seriously? If you told my husband that he was wired to be logical and I was wired to be emotional—that he needed respect and I needed love— he would wonder if you had gone off your meds. And it's not like we're some big exception to the rule. I know plenty of rational, steady-as-she-goes women, and plenty of off-the-walls emotional men. I bet you do too.

Honestly? Sometimes I think people are just making all that Mars and Venus stuff up to sell books.

So why do women hate on females? Why do we complain about our moody daughters, dragon bosses, and flaky selves?

Easy. The world has trained us to disdain womanhood. And rather than swim against the current of culture, defending our dignity and the dignity of our daughters, we've complied with society's low expectations (those generalizations we began to believe after constant exposure to them), allied ourselves with the dominant narrative (translation: we get a sense of power by saying demeaning things about ourselves before anyone else can, and from limiting ourselves in ways we know others will approve of), and sold ourselves and our sisters out in the process.

Not cool, moms. Not cool at all.

It's time to take back the narrative about women and girls.

I do think this is one of those things that is improving over time. As women are surpassing their brothers in educational attainment, excelling in the workplace, and managing to live healthy and successful lives with or without the help of Prince Charming, the myth of the hormonally imbalanced damsel in distress is beginning to wither away. (And can I just say, *anyone* would be emotionally volatile if they were forced to spend their entire life in an ivory tower.) But that damsel still rears her petulant head at times, and it's time to free our daughters, our sisters, and ourselves from her tyranny.

So. Stop generalizing about women. Stop complaining about how whiny your daughters are, or how bossy your boss is (ahem), or how flaky you are. Stop playing the hapless female (unless it's an emergency—I will admit that helpless females get their cars fixed faster). Stop viewing other women as your competition; stop criticizing, cutting down, and subtly undermining women who challenge you or make you feel inadequate. Claim the truth of who you are—a woman created in the very image of God—and stand strong, stand tall, stand proud. Stand for your daughters, for your sisters, for yourself, and for the glory of the God who created you.

Stand.

Give the Gift of Freedom from Slavery

For many people, the word "slavery" conjures up images of cotton plantations, slave ships, and whip-wielding villains in suspenders and felt hats. The United States was built as much on the backs of trafficked Africans as the dreams of European settlers, and it is important to remember that. But there is much more to slavery than that familiar stereotype. In fact, more people are living in slavery now than at any other time in human history. The vast majority of them are women and girls.

The Global Slavery Index, a report released by the anti-trafficking Walk Free Foundation, estimates that there are 35.8 million people living in modern-day slavery. It defines slavery as "one person possessing or controlling another person in such a way as to significantly deprive that person of their individual liberty, with the intention of exploiting that person through their use, management, profit, transfer, or disposal." This could include forced child labor, being trapped by debts owed to an employer or recruitment agent, or the exploitation of domestic workers.[10]

The form of modern slavery that has drawn the most attention recently is the sex industry. Millions of women and girls are enslaved and exploited, in brothels and on the streets, in massage parlors and suburban homes, in hotel rooms and video studios and strip clubs and spas. Even those who entered the sex trade willingly may have a hard time getting out (although some would argue that the fact that the average prostitute comes from a background rife with physical and sexual abuse, and entered the profession by age fourteen, calls the term "willingly" into question). Entrapment, addiction, social stigma, and lack of education or other options keep women stuck in the sex industry. When women do break free, many have no safe place to go and wind up right back where they started.

Ending this nightmare is going to take tremendous moral, social, and political will. But a simple way to begin to engage is by helping women who *do* break free and supporting the organizations that help them.

Here's an idea. Many nonprofits that work with survivors sell goods made by the women in their programs. This supports their ongoing work, teaches the women a trade, and provides survivors with a dignified source of income, whether they continue to work with the organization or establish their own shop. Most of the wares are focused on women—absolutely gorgeous jewelry, handbags, and scarves—because women resonate with their cause, and because survivors are often more comfortable interacting with female customers than male ones. So why not buy the women in your life goods made by sex trafficking survivors for the next gift-giving occasion? Dangly earrings from India, silk scarves from Thailand, a bracelet or clutch made in Kenya—your loved one gets a unique gift, survivors get a source of income, and you get to invest your Christmas budget in something that really matters, instead of blowing it at the mall. Win-win-win. Google the options, check the organizations out, and then shop until you drop a little hope into survivors' hearts.

Focus in on Teenage Girls

"Twelve to twenty-one is the danger zone for girls in our culture,"
I was chatting with Reverend Domnic Misolo, the director of the Ekklesia Foundation for Gender Education, as we stood in the lunch line, the hot Kenyan sun pounding down on our heads. I had traveled to East Africa to help train the teachers and clergy who would be launching a Bible-based youth curriculum I had written in Kenyan schools, but I was the one who was getting the education. Domnic went on to explain how teenage girls were often given away in marriage for dowry money; or lured into bad relationships by men who preyed on their low self-esteem; or left home to escape untenable family situations; or fell pregnant and dropped out of school, putting the dream of a healthy, stable future further from their reach.

My heart was broken as I learned about the barriers girls faced in sub-Saharan Africa, but I was also struck by how similar some of the struggles were to those of girls in the Western world. Dowries aside, we all know girls who were manipulated into an unhealthy relationship, or jumped out of the frying pan and into the fire trying to escape a miserable home life, or got pregnant and dropped out of school, locking themselves and their children into a cycle of poverty. Maybe we were that girl.

Twelve to twenty-one is the danger zone for girls in our culture as well.

Adolescence is difficult, a volatile stage of life where everything is in flux. Body. Emotions. Expectations. Sense of self. Ironically, it is during this tumultuous time that we begin to set the trajectory of our lives. What sort of relationships are we going to cultivate? Are we going to use substances like drugs and alcohol? How are we planning on supporting ourselves in our adult lives, and what role does education play in those plans? At what point are we going to become sexually active, and how are our choices in that area likely to affect our health and family status going forward? We may not like the fact that teenagers are struggling with those choices, but ignoring that reality won't make it go away.

To make matters worse, girls typically experience a drop in self-esteem and self-confidence when they hit adolescence, making it easier to fall prey to other people's plans for them—especially if that person seems likely to meet their psychosocial needs. It's easy to say yes (even when you'd rather say no), if that's the price of romance, friendship, and social inclusion.

As much as we'd like to protect girls from this, we really can't, and well-intentioned attempts to do so often backfire. What we can do is build them up, shoring up their confidence and sense of self so they can, hopefully, make wise decisions.

Pay attention to the teenage girls around you. Get to know them. Let them know you think that they are lovely human beings, worthy of respect. Ask for their thoughts and opinions on things, instead of just telling them yours. Whenever possible, present them with choices and leadership opportunities so they can practice making decisions and setting direction in a safe environment. Mentor them, modeling wise choices and good boundaries.

We can't protect girls from the challenges of adolescence, but we can walk with them through it. Focus in on teenage girls. You just might change a life.

Invest in Microfinance

Women in the developing world may be short on money, but that doesn't mean they're short on intellect, drive, and creativity. Sometimes all it takes for an impoverished mama to turn things around for her family is a hand up and a little leverage. Microfinance is an empowering way to help women build a better future for themselves and their families.

Around the world, the poorest of the poor don't have good access to financial services like savings accounts, insurance, and loans. I know, I know—we live in such an expensive, litigious, debt-saturated society that even thinking about those last two items makes us wince. But we're not talking about handing women a payday loan to buy a new pleather couch and a flat-screen TV. We're talking about loaning them a couple hundred dollars to buy seed, or cosmetics, or a sewing machine to start a small business; providing them with the ability to insure their business against catastrophic losses; and making sure they have a safe, secure place to keep their profits. Makes sense, right?

Here's the problem. The reason most banks don't provide loans to the very poor is because it is hard to make money off of them. The transaction costs alone—paying a bank employee to meet with the client, draw up the loan, and follow up with them on collections—can eat up a significant percentage of the money, particularly if they have to travel to far-flung areas to meet with the borrower. And then there's the cost of the loan itself. So microcredit sits in a strange place between business and charity, and isn't the best option for everyone. But for entrepreneurial mamas with a mind for business and a family to feed, it can make all the difference in the world.

So here's where you come in. You get to fund those loans! Many microfinance organizations crowdsource the money they lend out. Kiva is the organization most people are familiar with. It's an online hub that funnels money to a variety of microcredit lenders all around the world. You can go to their website, browse the borrowers, and give money toward a loan for a borrower you want to support. When the borrower has repaid the loan, you get the money back. You can reinvest the money in another borrower, donate it to Kiva, or withdraw the money and put it back in your own bank account.

Organizations like World Vision run their microfinance programs differently. They fund loans with donations, so when the borrower repays the loan, the money stays in the community and is available for other borrowers. You still get to browse the borrowers, catch their vision, and donate toward specific loans. You're just not going to get your ten, or fifty, or one hundred dollars back. You will get a nice tax deduction, though.

So go ahead. Hop online, get inspired by what women around the world are doing to build a better future for their families and communities, and lend a hand. What an exciting thing to be part of!

Because They Said So!

Bright Ideas from Mentor Moms

Invest in a good study Bible, and take the time to learn how to use many of the free resources available online. Check Bible dictionaries or commentaries out of your church library (or another church's library, if yours doesn't have one), and scour used bookstores for Christian classics. **How to Read the Bible for All Its Worth** *by Gordon D. Fee and Douglas Stuart is a fabulous primer that will sharpen your Bible study skills, and its companion,* **How to Read the Bible Book by Book,** *will give you a solid grasp of the entire Bible. Learning how to study the Bible on a deeper level is an investment you will never regret.*

—Jenny Rae Armstrong, mama of four

One of the most empowering things I ever did, and one I wish every woman could experience, was learning quality self-defense. The Rape Aggression Defense System (RAD) is phenomenal and uses compassionate, brave female instructors to help women overcome their fears and find confidence in their ability to protect themselves. This changed my life, and I support a friend who uses it in ministry to girls coming out of human trafficking. I watched a girl too nervous to even make eye contact transform in two months into a laughing, chattering bundle of energy. The body and soul are intimately connected; by strengthening one we can help heal the other.

—Natalie Nyquist, mama of one

Mighty Girl has so many book suggestions about girls and women who have made a difference. I give them to the girls in my life.

—Judy Douglass, mama of three

Watch the gender dynamics in the books you read and the media you consume. Many romance novels—even Christian ones—feature "alpha heroes" whose behavior is arrogant, controlling, and frankly abusive. This glorifies and normalizes un-Christlike behavior, recasting it as "romantic" and cultivating unhealthy appetites and expectations in the readers. It has a similar neurological and psychological effect to pornography, which conditions viewers to desire things that are not good for them or their partner. Dangerous, domineering, jealous heroes are not heroes at all. Pay attention to the messages you are allowing yourself and your children to be bombarded with.

—Jenny Rae Armstrong, mama of four

Our family connected with a ministry in Zambia that serves AIDS orphans and widows. After prayer, newsletters, orphan sponsorship, and several visits, we no longer call Every Orphan's Hope a mission partner—they are our friends. We know the names of dozens of orphans and numerous precious widows, and our children have been forever changed by their stories and their faith amidst adversity. God is so good!

—Sharon R. Hoover, mama of two

I have mentored young women, equipping them to use the gifts God has given them and helping them see their God-given value. My family reaches out to the single women in our congregation, who tend to be lonely, by inviting them over for a meal on a regular basis. We have also provided groceries and home-cooked meals for single moms.

—Leah Everson, mama of two

Engage your passion in a way that empowers underserved women. Afghan Women's Writing Project allows women writers in America to mentor up-and-coming women writers in in Afghanistan. If writing is not your passion, be blessed by reading the AWWP blog and be a blessing by leaving a comment for an aspiring writer.

—Margaret Philbrick, mama of three

Pay attention to how you compliment girls. As a child, I had waist-length blonde hair that everyone commented on. When my mother suggested cutting it to make it easier to handle, I blurted out "But then I won't be beautiful anymore!" I didn't work up the nerve to cut my hair until high school. Compliments can shape children powerfully, letting them know what we think is valuable and important about them. We tend to compliment girls on their appearance; let's try complimenting them on their compassion, or their work ethic, or their leadership skills instead.
—Jenny Rae Armstrong, mama of four

Mentor another mom from work, your neighborhood, or church. Take note of someone who is hurting, struggling, or wounded, especially another mom who lacks confidence and wisdom in raising her own children but sincerely wants help. By setting a regular time to meet, you can set boundaries and be clear on expectations. Use the mode of communication you are most familiar with: meeting face to face, talking on the phone, texting, or video chatting. Discuss allowances, chores, discipline, and childhood diets, as well as how to help a child spiritually.
—JoHannah Reardon, mama of three

Notes

[1] M. C. Black, K. C. Basile, M. J. Breiding, S. G. Smith, M. L. Walter, M. T. Merrick, J. Chen, and M. R. Stevens, *The National Intimate Partner and Sexual Violence Survey (NISVS): Summary Report* (Atlanta, GA: National Center for Injury Prevention and Control, Centers for Disease Control and Prevention, 2011).

[2] "The Girl Effect Fact Sheet," www.girleffect.org/media/1470/ge_infographic -the-girl-effect-factsheet_download.pdf (accessed October 19, 2015).

[3] Susan Mayor, "Pregnancy and Childbirth Are Leading Causes of Death in Teenage Girls in Developing Countries," BMJ Publishing Group, 2004, www .ncbi.nlm.nih.gov/pmc/articles/PMC411126.

[4] "The Girl Effect Fact Sheet," www.girleffect.org/media/1470/ge_infographic -the-girl-effect-factsheet_download.pdf (accessed October 19, 2015).

[5] "Educate Girls, Fight AIDS," The Global Coalition on Women and AIDS, http://data.unaids.org/gcwa/gcwa_fs_girlseducation_sep05_en.pdf (accessed October 19, 2015).

[6] M. C. Black et al., 2011.

[7] Steven R. Tracy, "Patriarchy and Domestic Violence: Challenging Common Misconceptions," *Journal of the Evangelical Theological Society*, 50(3), 581.

[8] *State of the World's Mothers 2014* (Fairfield, CT: Save the Children, 2014).

[9] Nicholas Kristof, "A Tipping Point on Maternal Mortality?" *New York Times* blog, July 30, 2009, http://kristof.blogs.nytimes.com/2009/07/30/a-tipping -point-on-maternal-mortality/?_r=0.

[10] *The Global Slavery Index 2014*, Hope for Children Organization Australia, 2014, http://d3mj66ag9ob5fy.cloudfront.net/wp-content/uploads/2014/11 /Global_Slavery_Index_2014_final_lowres.pdf.

POWER OUTLET EIGHT

Work It, Mama!

Growing up, I was convinced I was going to be a stay-at-home mom. I loved kids and found the idea of a cozy, domestic life incredibly appealing. I could be like those pretty Amish ladies in Christian romance novels! I envisioned myself baking bread, canning produce from my organic garden, and reading to an adoring posse of cherubic children until my husband came home from his oh-so-stable nine-to-five job.

And then I actually *became* a stay-at-home mom. Ha!

There's a tendency to romanticize homemaking in Christian circles. It's a big, scary world out there, and we like things that conjure up images of security and safety—that remind us of simpler times when all we had to worry about was starvation, dysentery, and our sole provider getting shot while massacring the people we stole our land from.

Okay, sorry. You can see why I totally failed at the Amish housewife thing.

No matter how much we love our children and enjoy home-making, motherhood and all its trappings are only part of who we are, part of what God created us to do and be. They're a good part, certainly. A wonderful part. But the idea that being a wife and mom is a woman's highest calling is a bunch of unbiblical malarkey. Our highest calling, our *only* calling, is to be a follower of Christ. Everything else needs to flow out of that, or risk becoming an idol.

This section is about vocation, about the work God has prepared for us and equipped us to do. It doesn't matter if you're a career woman, a stay-at-home mom, or something in between; we all have passions and skills that can be put to good use for the kingdom. Maybe your mad crafting abilities could turn a profit, and you could give the proceeds to charity. Maybe you could put that master's in English to work tutoring ESL students at the local library. Maybe you could stop looking at your job as a diversion from God's plan (well, your plan, actually) for your life, lean in, and glorify God by becoming the best accountant/waitress/software developer/customer service rep you can possibly be. Same goes for stay-at-home moms pining for the days of team meetings and watercooler conversations. What might God want to do in and through your work?

In Genesis, we see that work is a good thing, something God created human beings to do. Ask God what he has for you to do today, and then work at it with all your heart. Whatever it is. Wherever you are. For the good of the kingdom and the glory of God.

Work it, mama!

Stop Wasting Your Time

As moms, we have a lot on our plate. Juggling schedules, maintaining a household, and making sure the kids are clean, fed, and reasonably happy can suck up as much time as we give it, not to mention any responsibilities we have on top of that. We also have dreams and passions all our own: that book we want to write, that degree we want to finish, those running shoes collecting dust in the back of our closet.

It's easy to fall back on the excuse that we don't have time; and sometimes, that's true. Sometimes, we have to make sacrifices for the good of others or for our own mental health. But the fact remains: this is the twenty-first century. We get to make choices, and the things that we have decided need to get done, get done. Hiding behind your family, citing them as the reason you're unable to accomplish all those things you want to do in life, is as bad for you as it is for them. Don't give in to the martyr complex!

Obviously, I'm not saying that you should neglect your kids to pursue your dreams (although I am here to tell you, sending store-bought cupcakes to school on your child's birthday or making your middle schooler wash their own clothes does not constitute neglect). I am suggesting that you get strategic about your time management. There are only twenty-four hours in a day, and if we want to carve out space for our neglected passions, we are going to have to stop doing some things.

Start by taking a good, hard look at your media consumption. A Nielsen report from 2014 revealed some startling statistics: the average adult in the United States spends nearly three hours a day listening to the radio, five and a half hours watching television, an hour on their smartphone, and an hour surfing the Web on their computer.[1] That's nearly eleven hours per day, for those of you who are keeping track. Granted, people are probably doing other things while they're listening to the radio. And I suspect that if you removed baby boomers and their elderly parents from the mix, the ratio of television to smartphone/Internet usage would be reversed. I don't know about you, but I don't even watch TV on my TV anymore. Still, the point remains. The average American spends a ridiculous amount of time staring at screens.

I have a theory about why that is. I think we get online because we are lonely and bored, and we watch TV because we are tired. The problem is, those activities (if they can be called that) only make us more lonely, bored, and tired than we were in the first place, while sucking up time that could be devoted to real things in our lives. Good, hard, glorious things like taking our kids on a brisk walk around the neighborhood, or pulling out our paints, or catching up on those things that are stressing us out, or filling out that college application.

Digital media is killing our dreams, damaging our relationships, and stealing our precious time, one reality show, game app, and status update at a time. It's time to pull the plug and reclaim our lives.

A word to the wise: if you decide to cut back on your media consumption to pursue things you are passionate about, don't expect those hours to translate directly. If you usually veg out in front of the TV after supper with the kids crawling all over you, that's probably not the time to start working on your novel. Work on your novel in the morning, and do the housework you would have done then during the TV hours. It will take some time to figure out what works for you, but once you do, go with it!

Don't let your technology go all Terminator on your dreams, and stop using your family as an excuse. Get ruthless about cutting out things that are wasting your time, and do those things that God created you to do.

Pay Attention to the People around You

It must have been strange for Jesus, walking this earth he created with the people he had come to save. What thoughts were running through his mind as he experienced the beauty and depravity of humanity at ground level, so to speak? I can't help but wonder how Jesus looked at people—what his expression was like when he accused the Pharisees, or blessed the children, or raised the widow's son, or interacted with the Syrophoenician woman. How did people feel in his presence? Could they tell that there was something different about him by the way he interacted with those around him?

It begs the question: How do people feel in our presence? Can they tell that there is something different about us by the way we interact with those around us?

I'm sure we've all known those people who just radiate warmth, or gentleness, or hospitality, or Spirit-filled confidence. Like Snow White, they tend to have an entourage, and can usually be found at the center of a group of young children, doe-eyed adults who hang on their every word, and small woodland creatures. There is something different about these folks, something that attracts people to them. And after long consideration, I think I know why that is.

I think it is because they look at people the way Jesus looks at them. I think it is because they radiate deep, selfless love and focused attention, and respond to those around them with remarkable compassion. And everyone is hungry for that kind of Jesus-y love, whether they realize it or not.

So what does this have to do with vocation? While people may hope to experience that sort of care and consideration at home or even at church, they don't usually expect to encounter it in the marketplace. But your coworkers need Jesus. Your clients need Jesus. Your boss needs Jesus, and the man waiting your table needs Jesus, and the girl checking your groceries needs Jesus. And you might be the only Jesus they see.

Every morning before you roll out of bed, ask God to give you his heart for people. Ask him to help you see them as he sees them, and love them as he loves them. Then, as you go throughout your day, pay attention to the people you interact with. Remind yourself that they are beloved of God, and that they have their own deep stories and histories and lives, full of joy and pain and victories and frailties. The barista at the Starbucks near your office does not exist to mix your caramel macchiato; she is sacred, a bearer of God's image, and Jesus spilled his blood for love of her. There is no such thing as an ordinary person, and remembering that could transform the way you interact with the people around you, how you perceive them, and how they perceive you.

Pay attention. If you keep your eyes open and look for the wonder, and the beauty, and the transformation of the people around you, you just might find it.

Tie on an Apron and Work for Charity

My friend Nancy does housekeeping for missionaries. No, she doesn't fly over to Uganda and scrub their shower stalls. She spends a couple hours a week cleaning and running errands for an elderly woman in her community, and uses the proceeds to support missionaries.

Now, Nancy wouldn't need to do housework for anyone. She lives in a huge, tastefully decorated house on a lake. Her husband makes a lot of money, and she still subs at the private school where she taught for years. She could easily write a check and be done with it. But housecleaning is her way of getting tangibly involved in a cause that she cares about.

The missionaries are not the only ones who benefit. When I was staying with Nancy for a few days, I went with her to visit the lady she cleans for, a stooped widow with a first-generation Scandinavian accent. Nancy listened to her concerns about her latest medications, made plans to pick her up for the Norwegian Christmas service at a church a few towns over, and offered to pick up lunch from Hardee's. En route to the drive-through, Nancy fretted about the neglected appearance of the woman's garage door, and decided to spruce it up so local hoodlums wouldn't figure out that a little old lady lived there by herself. Clearly, Nancy wasn't in it for the money. An elderly widow got a friend and protector, missionaries got funds to support vital ministries, and Nancy got the satisfaction of doing something tangible for the kingdom of God.

Could you pick up some domestic work to bless others? Maybe there's a wheelchair-bound woman in your church who needs a hand when her husband is working the night shift, a mom who needs childcare one afternoon a week, or an elderly neighbor who needs someone to keep their walkways clear in winter. Check with social service agencies and home healthcare providers in your community to get connected with people who need housemaids, caregivers, or companions for a few hours a week. It may wind up being a blessing, in more ways than one.

Keep Your Skills Sharp

The mommy wars are over. While there are still pockets of resistance in the extreme sides of each camp, most people's opinions about whether women should pursue a career or focus their full energies on homemaking have softened under the onslaught of real life (thank goodness). About 30 percent of mothers stay home with their kids,[2] a third work part time,[3] and the rest are employed full time.

Do you know what that means? It means that whichever choice you've made is completely average. That's kind of comforting, right? It also means that statistically speaking, even if you are in full-on stay-at-home-mom mode, you'll probably enter the work force at some point. That may be comforting or terrifying, depending on your perspective. In any case, keeping your skills sharp can help you face the future with confidence and enable a smoother transition into the workforce, if and when you do go back.

If you had a career or specialization before becoming a mother—if you were a nurse, or a systems analyst, or worked in advertising—stay up to date with what is happening in your industry. Keep your licenses current. Subscribe to trade magazines or relevant blogs. If there is a way to volunteer your skills or work very part time, give it some serious consideration. It will keep your skills fresh and look good on your résumé.

If you're still not sure what you want to be when you grow up, now is a good time to explore that. Consider your strengths and weaknesses, your likes and dislikes, now that you're not eighteen and boy crazy. Read up on the options, and talk to your friends about their jobs. I know many moms who went back to school (on campus or online) when their babies did—in fact, I was one of them. It's easier to do when you're not giving up a pre-existing source of income, and school is often more flexible than employment, making for a smoother transition. Plus, many schools can assist with job placement once you've finished your course of study.

Don't get me wrong. Soak up every second you get with your babies, and don't waste this season pining for a different one. But your kids are not in competition with your career. Keeping your skills sharp will benefit you all in the long run, and just might keep you sane in the interim.

Create a Triple Threat

When I was tiny, I adored *Sesame Street*. The letters. The music. Those goofy, gentle monsters. Then one day, I saw a ballerina twirling across the screen, and knew I had found my calling in life. I ran into the kitchen and informed my mother that I was going to be a ballerina when I grew up.

Needless to say, my life didn't turn out that way, but it wasn't just a preschooler's passing fancy, either. I took dance lessons whenever my family could afford it, taught baby ballet as a high schooler, and, until a massive purging spree last year, could always pull a black leotard and pink tights out of my dresser (just in case the Sugar Plum Fairy sprained her ankle or something, and this thirty-something mama of four was called upon to dance the part, right?). My father's efforts to get me interested in sports failed miserably. It was all dance, all the time, with a side of music and theater.

Yep, I was one of them. If you are too, read on.

One of the cool things about the church is that it is one of the last week-to-week bastions of the performing arts. Some people cringe at the idea of "performance" in church, but the arts are an incredible way to worship God. One of King David's first courses of action upon bringing the Ark of the Covenant back to Jerusalem was to hire a bunch of professional musicians to get the party started, and keep it going morning and evening, into perpetuity. So no hating on artists in church! It's biblical!

The vast majority of churches have some sort of music ministry, and some utilize drama and dance in their worship services. Are there ways you can plug in to the artistic ministries already happening at your church? I attended a decade of worship practices with a baby in a sling; my shoulders didn't love it, but the babies enjoyed the music, and the team members adored the babies. Other churches would love to use drama and dance effectively in worship, but need someone who knows how to pull that off. Could that someone be you?

Even if there aren't places for you to get involved in Sunday morning worship, consider using your passion for music, dance, or theater with the kids in your church and community. Could you organize a children's choir, coach kids doing skits for junior church, or help with the annual Christmas pageant? If you're really ambitious, see if the church would let you offer a free guitar class or a homeschool chorale in their facilities. Or get involved in community theater (some are great about providing opportunities for kids to perform with their parents) and see how God uses you there. Get creative about ways you can use your gifts to engage your community and glorify God. Then, go out and break a leg!

Coach the Team

I'll never forget that one year when my kids played soccer. It was a summer league that practiced two times per week, all the different age groups spread out across the middle school's football field like an invading horde of halflings in knee socks. I had one kid in U-5, one in U-8, one in U-10, and one in U-14. It was a madhouse.

But what really got me was the fact that two of the teams my kids were on asked me to consider coaching. After I picked my very un-athletic jaw up off the ground, I explained that I was only broiling myself on this football field for love of my children, and was the very last person they wanted coaching anything that didn't involve vocal scales or pirouettes. They assured me that no experience was necessary, and that they would train anyone who was willing to help.

I still said no, but wow. What an incredible opportunity for parents who don't hate sports!

Coaches can have an amazing impact on the kids they work with. Getting to spend several hours a day investing in kids' lives, several days a week during the course of the season, is an opportunity that would turn many pastors green with envy. In fact, I know quite a few pastors who coach on the side for exactly that reason. The best coaches aren't just trying to build a winning team, or show kids how to get the ball in the goal; they are trying to instill the values of hard work, perseverance, and cooperation into their charges.

Coaches often develop a relationship with their team members' families too. I have a friend whose husband considers coaching his ministry; as a familiar, trusted figure who is vested in their child, he is the first person many of them turn to in a crisis, particularly if they don't have a church or extended family nearby. You want to reach out to the single moms, the fatherless, and the outsiders in your community? Coaching will put you in close contact with many of them.

If your kids are involved in sports anyway, coaching is a huge win-win: a way for you to connect with your children, invest in your community, and keep your own skills sharp while enjoying the game. So what are you waiting for, coach? Head down to the YMCA, fill out a volunteer application, and get the ball rolling.

Mentoring and Mothering

By Natasha Sistrunk Robinson

Christian moms sure do enjoy their holy huddles. Before I became a mom, I was not welcomed by these women; and once I became a mom, I didn't want to isolate myself in that way. After all, besides being mothers, we didn't have much in common. I worked full time as an active-duty military officer, regularly traveled for work, led a diverse women's small group at my church, and wrote or mentored college students in my "spare time." There was no room in my life for playdates I wouldn't enjoy and that my daughter wouldn't remember anyway, so I took a pass.

I didn't fit the mold. The only reason I was okay with that was because God was already working in my heart, affirming my identity in him through his Word and through significant mentoring relationships. Because my mentors were quite diverse—young and old, male and female, and from various racial and ethnic backgrounds—I continued to draw strength, encouragement, and direction from them as a young, professional mom living her life with purpose for God.

As someone who has spent years mentoring women at various life stages, I regularly hear concerns about losing one's self in marriage and motherhood. I have counseled people to remember that a woman who loses herself so easily might not have her eyes fixed in the right direction. Instead of seeing motherhood as a force crashing in on all your hopes and dreams, consuming your life with mundane tasks, ask yourself, "How might God use this, even this responsibility of motherhood, to affirm my identity in him? How can motherhood give me an opportunity to fix my eyes on Jesus?"

Now that my daughter is eight years old, allow me to let you in on a crazy thought: she has mentored me. When I submit to her in the simplest of ways, especially when I don't want to, I am reminded of Christ, the suffering servant. When I humble myself to consider her needs or give her the last cookie (sometimes), I am reminded of my need to confess my selfish desires. In the quiet task of prayer and intercession for her and the souls of her friends (who will have influence in her life as she continues to grow and trust them), I learn discipline and perseverance in my faith. I know she is quick to forgive, so when I say, "Mommy screwed up; I'm sorry. Will you forgive me?" it reminds me of Christ's love and sacrifice for me, and my need to quickly forgive others. I am my daughter's primary mentor, assigned by God, but I need her to teach and train me as well.

As a young mom, I was intentional about continuing my relationships with the diverse group of mentors God had placed in my life. I encourage you to expand your community, and avoid losing yourself in the mommy huddle. Our primary vocation and calling in this life is to make disciples of Jesus. That is our top priority, as mothers of our children, and with anyone else God has given us the privilege of influencing. Godly mentors remind us of this priority so our world does not revolve around our home, our family, and our children. Dirty dishes? No worries. Stained carpet? Who cares? Children need to see their mothers partnering with brothers and sisters to engage the world for Christ. This is how we best love them. This is how we don't lose ourselves. This is how we raise up the next generation of Christ followers.

Natasha Sistrunk Robinson is author of Mentor for Life: Finding Purpose through Intentional Discipleship. *She is also founder and president of Leadership LINKS. Connect with Natasha through her official website at www.natashasrobinson.com or* A Sista's Journey *blog at www.asistasjourney .com.*

Grow a Garden

Ah, gardening. The first and most necessary human vocation. Most of us have gotten pretty out of touch with where our food comes from, which is too bad, since gardening is a great way to regain a sense of balance in a world that seems to have gone off its rocker. If you already garden, you know what I'm talking about. If you don't, here are six reasons I think everyone should try gardening: in your yard, on your patio, on your windowsill, or in the local community garden.

IT'S GOOD FOR YOU

In our modern world, many of us try to relieve stress by watching TV, or taking a bubble bath, or having a glass of wine. Sometimes that helps, but usually, it's exactly the wrong strategy. Exercising your body while doing something productive is much more effective. Getting out in the sunshine and plunging your hands in the dirt, planting seeds and pulling weeds, is an amazing stress reliever. It's almost like we're doing what we were created to do, or something.

IT'S GOOD FOR YOUR KIDS

Children today have become very detached from the natural world, and it is simply not healthy, for them or for our world. Gardening is a great first step in teaching them about the natural balance of the world God created, and how to steward it well. Give them their own patch of dirt, and let them plant crooked rows, "weed" out seedlings, and stain their clothes with soil. The look of pride on a preschooler's face when they pull their first carrot out of the ground is worth it all. And bonus: kids are much more willing to try vegetables that they grew themselves.

IT SAVES MONEY

Don't get me wrong; if you're not careful, you could easily drop large wads of cash in a greenhouse or gardening center. But if you stick to simple veggies that grow well in your climate, and don't feel the need to get down and dirty among birdbaths, gazing globes, and plaster-of-paris fairy statues, all you need are a pair of sturdy gloves, a few simple tools, and a handful of gardening stakes. Learning how to store or preserve vegetables means your garden could save you money all year long, not just during the summer.

IT KEEPS CHEMICALS OFF YOUR PLATE

Gardening puts you in control of your food (within reason, of course). You know exactly where it came from and what chemicals have or have not been used. Also, did we mention saving money? If you're one of those people who pays extra to buy organic produce, think of the other ways you could use the money you save.

IT TASTES BETTER

Enough said. There is simply no comparison between a tomato or snap pea or cucumber fresh from your garden, still warm from the sun, and the kind you buy at the grocery store. If you have never popped a cherry tomato straight off the vine and into your mouth, you have simply never lived.

YOU CAN SHARE YOUR SURPLUS

The only time people at my church lock their car doors is during zucchini season. Otherwise, you never know how many bags of veggies will be abandoned in your backseat! While we joke about it, having enough fresh produce to share with your neighbors is one of the benefits of gardening. A paper grocery bag filled with garden goodies is an incredible way to nourish people's bodies *and* hearts.

Turn Your Passion into Profit— for Someone Else

Okay, I'm just gonna say it. Being a mom can be boring. Mothering is a whirl of activity, yes, but not exactly the kind that engages the full powers of our intellect and creativity. It's important to have some sort of outlet, for your own mental health if nothing else. But have you thought about ways your skills, passions, and expertise could benefit your community?

Many people get a tremendous sense of satisfaction out of creating things that are beautiful, practical, and tangible. I have one friend who makes the most gorgeous mittens out of upcycled sweaters, and one who makes soaps, lotions, and natural cosmetics. There's this woman from my home church who carves exquisite utensils out of scraps of wood, and another who spins yarn from natural wool. I know painters and seamstresses and jewelry makers and woodworkers galore—and that's just within a one-mile radius of my house!

If you have a passion for creating beautiful things, consider how that could be used to benefit others. The money you make selling your handmade earrings on Etsy may not be enough to impact your bottom line, but it could make all the difference for a mama in the developing world struggling to support her kids. When my grandma was recovering from her stroke, she and my aunt would crochet granny squares to be turned into bedspreads for the local women's shelter. The women and children could take them with them when they left, a homemade reminder that someone was thinking of them and cheering them on. I knew one little girl who organized a monthly crafting circle with her friends. They hawked their wares at church and gave their considerable profits to charity.

We're not all crafty, but we're all good at something. Can I be honest for a minute? Most churches rely on women for providing the snacks, and staffing the children's ministry, and making sure the building looks good, but suffer from a serious lack of imagination about what could be accomplished if women were let loose on other tasks. Finance. Web design. Marketing. Social media management. These are all things most nonprofits need, and that moms can do from home while their kids are napping. Pastors are often expected to function as social workers or counselors, especially in low-income or rural areas, but if you happen to have an *actual* background in counseling or social work? You have no idea how much your pastor could use your help.

Are you a nurse, or paralegal, or military officer? Are you a whiz with a camera, or drywall tape, or computers? What do you enjoy doing—either because it's fun, or simply because you're so good at it? Get creative about ways you could use your skills to benefit your church, your community, and your world.

Because They Said So!

Bright Ideas from Mentor Moms

Working outside of the home does not negate your ministry inside of the home. In fact, it can expand it. When you can, talk to your children about your work and who you are helping through your job. Include them when you can; take them to the office or have them join you for an event. Talk to them about the dignity of work and encourage them to consider how they might help or minister to others outside the home, too—and then join them in those pursuits!
—Ann Swindell, mama of one

I work closely with a nonprofit in East Palo Alto that empowers young single mothers by giving them the opportunity to be trained in areas that are highly employable here in the Bay Area, such as SEO, e-commerce, Website design, photography, and marketing. As an artist, I use my gifts to teach the mothers new, physical art skills to create salable products. I am also helping the organization design and vision their physical workspace. It's near and dear to my heart and I love helping these mamas!
—Janine Crum, mama of two

Moms put in a lot of work that is not necessarily valued by others. Do yourself the service of taking your unpaid work seriously, whether you are scrubbing the bathtub, toiling away on the novel you're writing, going grocery shopping with the kids, or helping your grandma balance her checkbook. Get dressed every day in clothes that make you feel good (even if it's just a flattering pair of yoga pants and a cute tee), put on shoes, and arrange your hair into some semblance of order. Set short-term and long-term goals, and make a list of the things you want to accomplish the next day before you go to bed at night. If you drag around in PJs all day, with no direction and plan, you are going to feel crummy. Respect yourself and the work that you do, and make sure your subconscious gets the message that you mean business.

    —Jenny Rae Armstrong, mama of four

Don't feel guilty about carving out time to pursue your passion. Make a plan to leave the house, lock yourself in a room, or whatever it takes to regularly do what God's given you a fire for. Put it on the calendar.

    —Erin F. Wasinger, mama of three

Have you heard of plarn? The whole world of "plastic yarn" blew me away when I learned about it several years ago. I recycle my plastic grocery bags by cutting them into strips and creating plarn. With a huge hook, I crochet 4' x 6' sleeping mats for the homeless people in our community. Friends and family help by saving grocery bags and even making plarn for me. I get to use my love of handcrafts, and my family gets involved in caring for our vulnerable neighbors.

    —Sharon R. Hoover, mama of two

Having trouble figuring out what job to take or what direction to go? Make your decisions using the umbrella of the Bible and the Holy Spirit. Will this work help me be the kind of mom and person the Bible says we should be, or will it pull me away from that? Take time to pray and listen to the nudges of the Holy Spirit. When you pray, do you feel excitement or peace, or do you feel as if God is yelling no?

    —JoHannah Reardon, mama of three

I have used my nursing skills to help at a church health fair and help friends navigate questions about their illnesses and diagnoses. My perspective as a part-time working mom (a clinical nurse specialist) has given me the opportunity to engage in conversations with others at church that they say "sharpened" them. In general, the knowledge and confidence I gain in the workforce spills over into every aspect of my life. I see it all as kingdom work; there needn't be a dividing line.

    —Heidi Wheeler, mama of four

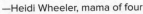

Notes

[1] *The Total Audience Report December 2014*, The Nielsen Company, 2014, http://ir.nielsen.com/files/doc_presentations/2014/The-Total-Audience-Report.pdf.

[2] D'Vera Cohn, Gretchen Livingston, and Wendy Wang, "After Decades of Decline, A Rise in Stay-at-Home Mothers," Pew Research Center, April 8, 2014, www.pewsocialtrends.org/2014/04/08/after-decades-of-decline-a-rise-in-stay-at-home-mothers.

[3] Diana Lavery, "More Mothers of Young Children in U.S. Workforce," Population Reference Bureau, www.prb.org/Publications/Articles/2012/us-working-mothers-with-children.aspx (accessed October 30, 2015).

POWER OUTLET NINE

The Church Ladies: From Holy Huddle to Full-Court Press

Remember Dana Carvey's Church Lady character from *Saturday Night Live*? That prim and proper scold who hid her control issues under a veil of religiosity? Even within the church, "church ladies" have sometimes earned the reputation of being cliquey, impossible-to-please women who care more about putting on the perfect brunch than about the people they are serving. That stereotype has caused more than one woman to shy away from female-led activities in the church. I understand, but I still think it's an absolute tragedy.

Here's the thing. You can find "church ladies" of the Dana Carvey variety, both male and female, in any organization. And if women have traditionally ranked higher on the passive aggression scale, perhaps that's because they were trying to get stuff done in systems where women who were upfront about their thoughts, opinions, and preferences were treated like Jezebels. And there is no question—church ladies got stuff done.

But praise God, we don't need to play those games anymore. We were never called to participate in that cultural nonsense in the first place. What we are called to do is move forward in love and power and self-discipline, functioning as Jesus' hands and feet in this world. And we are not called to do it alone.

I think it's very telling that in the New Testament, you rarely hear of people doing ministry by themselves. They went out in groups of two or more, and even the hermit-like John the Baptist and Jesus himself traveled with an entourage. Moses and Elijah may have taken solitary treks into the wilderness, but God sent people to come alongside them in their ministry when they were getting discouraged. It begs the question: If the mightiest heroes of the faith didn't try to go it alone in their calling, why do we?

The job is simply too big for us to take on alone, the opposition too discouraging. We need our brothers and sisters in Christ to help us and encourage us along the way. We need—brace yourselves—the church. And not just in the cosmic, all-Christians-are-the-church sense. I'm talking about those aggravating people who meet on Sunday mornings in that musty building down the road.

The local church, warts and all, is God's strategy for changing the world. This section is about how you can partner with other women from your local congregation to make a difference in your community, no plastic doilies or Jell-O molds required.

Throw a Back-to-School Bash

I am incredibly thankful for the American public school system. While it has its issues, the fact that every child has the right to an education and a school that is responsible to provide it to them is an improvement over the situation in many parts of the world. But hoo boy. Anyone who thinks public school is free has obviously not looked at the back-to-school supply lists my kids' district puts out!

School supplies can get pricey, and it's not unusual for teachers to use their own money to buy supplies for students whose parents can't or won't provide them. And let's be real—while some people adore it, there are few things more migraine-inducing than back-to-school shopping, especially when you're juggling multiple lists. I mean, picture me in Walmart, four boys swarming my cart, trying to make sure everyone has the correct ratio of pencil-top erasers and glue sticks while breaking up fights over Spiderman folders and presiding over a full-scale inquisition on which kid needs to use the bathroom.

So not my thing.

Why not kill several birds with one graphing calculator and host a back-to-school festival at your church?

There are many ways you could do this, so I am going to give you some à la carte options to discuss with your team.

GATHER YOUR SUPPLIES

Get the back-to-school shopping lists for the schools in your area and go from there. You could set out boxes at your church and collect whatever school supplies people happen to bring; make a list of the supplies you want to provide and have people sign up to purchase them; hit local businesses up for donations; get the back-to-school bash written into your church's outreach budget; or just ask people to write checks and then go shopping, at a bricks and mortar store or online. Personally, I'd suggest keeping a tight reign on the inventory. It makes the whole process less chaotic. Have a suggested donation for partygoers who just want to avoid shopping, but make sure struggling families know everything's available for free.

PLAN THE PARTY

Some churches collect the supplies and give them directly to the school, which is great, but not as much fun. Throw a big party, and invite everyone in the neighborhood! Make sure you have food and snacks—church ladies are great at that, right? Rent a bouncy house, recruit some teenagers to do face painting, and set up fun carnival games for the kids to play. Get someone from the local Christian radio station to come and broadcast live, or have your youth band prepare a few sets. Make it fun, and get everyone in your church involved.

ORGANIZE THE DISTRIBUTION

Decide how to distribute the school supplies at the party. Are you going to pre-pack backpacks by grade and gender, and hand them to the kids on the way out? Are you going to lay the supplies out on tables, and let kids pick what they want? One church I went to gave the supplies out as prizes for the carnival games; kids could win a notebook at the ring toss, or a pack of crayons at the fishing pool. Or give each kid a list of everything they need, based on their grade and school, and send them on a scavenger hunt around the church!

There are so many creative ways your church can reach out to the families in your community and make back-to-school preparations a little less stressful. Have fun with it!

Take the Kids to a Nursing Home

Some of my earliest memories involve visiting my Great-Grandma Anna at the Nopeming Nursing Home near Duluth, Minnesota. A funny, feisty lady with a thick Norwegian accent, she would juice me up on milky coffee, feed me sugar lumps straight from the dish, and then make me stand up and perform for all her friends.

You can see why I turned out the way I did.

Grandma Anna loved our visits, and so did I. I was six when she died, and I coped with this first brush with death by going outside, gathering the prettiest autumn leaves I could find, and informing the grown ups that they were for inside grandma's casket. They honored my request, and it still makes me happy to think of Grandma Anna resting with a little girl's crumpled, soil-stained offering of love.

Why do we keep children and the elderly apart, when each offers a perspective the other so desperately needs?

Nursing homes can be sad, lonely places, and even the best ones are incredibly boring. Bringing kids in for a visit can break up the monotony and lift the mood. I know, I know. Descending on a local nursing home with a brood of energetic children might seem like a recipe for disaster. But a little strategic planning goes a long way toward making sure everyone ends up with a smile on their faces.

If your church already has connections in a local nursing home, start there. Talk to the activities director about the best times to visit and what activities the residents might enjoy doing with the kids. Music is always a big favorite, and many older people light up when they hear Sunday school songs they sang as children. But don't stop there. Older children can perform skits. Teens may enjoy giving the residents manicures. Younger kids will find a rapt audience to practice their budding reading skills on.

Personally, I think that crafting is one of the most underrated nursing home activities, especially since children's and seniors' fine motor skills often operate at a similar level. Pairing kids and seniors up for simple craft projects gives them plenty of reason and opportunity to interact, and keeps the kids focused on an activity other than running up and down the halls. Holiday-themed projects are especially meaningful. Projects like creating valentines out of paper doilies, dying Easter eggs, making handprint turkeys out of colored paper, and decorating Christmas cookies conjure up good memories for many seniors and give them back a little of what time and infirmity has taken from them.

Could you load up the kids from your church and take them to a local nursing home once a month? The residents would adore it, the kids would gain new friends who are very different from them, and you would get the chance to bless some of society's more sidelined and forgotten people.

Just don't let them juice the kids up on coffee and sugar lumps.

Embrace Families With Special Needs

"Discipline begins in the home, dear."

My eyes welled with tears, and I bundled up my precious toddler and rushed out of the church, away from the frowning nursery worker. My firstborn had always been an easy baby, a curly-headed cherub with a striking resemblance to the Gerber baby. But things began to change when he was about sixteen months old, and I was starting to see the behavior the nursery worker described at home too.

Jamison had ignored the other kids and headed straight for the potted ficus, plunging his chubby little hands into the soil and flinging it everywhere.

Jamison had dumped the bucket of Legos over his head instead of playing with them nicely.

Jamison refused to listen to the nursery workers, or even meet their eyes, and would hit, kick, or bite anyone who got too close, especially if they were trying to redirect him. Sometimes, he would clap his hands over his ears and start screaming for no discernible reason.

Of course, most of you twenty-first-century mommies are clutching your pearls (or your Ugandan paper bead necklace) and thinking, "That baby has autism." And you're right. In fact, he's a wonderful young man now, and he *still* has autism. But back in the 1990s, the autism epidemic was just getting started, and few people were familiar with the signs. So my son's bizarre behaviors were chalked up to a lack of discipline in the home (read: the eighteen-month-old liked to twist himself up in the curtains because his mom didn't spank him enough). So at the point in my life when I was the most broken, and terrified, and in desperate need of help and support from the community of faith, I got judgment and isolation instead.

Look, I am just going to say this. Raising a child with special needs is hard. I know parents of kids with special needs are supposed to be heroic and brave and write inspiring blog posts and Instagram goofy pictures of their special little angel. We do that because we want you to know how much we adore our kids, and (real talk) because we don't want you to get an abortion if prenatal testing shows that there's something wrong with your child. That your kid might be like ours. We also do it because it makes you more comfortable to think of us as super parents who have been blessed with some magical ability to cope with circumstances that scare your pants off. But we aren't, we haven't been, and it's hard. We wouldn't trade our babies for anything, but it's hard.

It's also incredibly isolating. Many daycares, church nurseries, and friends-whose-houses-we-used-to-frequent are not well equipped to deal with kids with special needs. But oh, church. We need to do better. What does it say when we turn away the child with cerebral palsy because our Sunday school teachers find their disabilities daunting? When disabled adults are seen as a problem because their mere presence makes people uncomfortable? When the young mom leaves every week in tears, because the frazzled nursery workers make it clear that there is either something very wrong with her baby or something very wrong with her parenting, and she's not sure which is worse?

Why does the church reject and isolate those vulnerable souls who most desperately need her love, compassion, and care?

Churches need to welcome people with special needs and their families. Trust me, I am aware of how difficult this is. But it can be done. Will you be an advocate for these precious children and their families in your church? The next Bright Idea will give you some ideas on how to do that.

How to Embrace Families with Special Needs

Hopefully the previous Bright Idea convinced you of the importance of welcoming kids with special needs and their families into your church. Here are a few tangible ways to get started.

DON'T JUDGE THE PARENTS

It's so easy to demonize or lionize the parents of children with special needs in an attempt to make sense of the disability. Either they did something to mess their child up (this could be anything from abuse to vaccinations to not eating enough oranges during pregnancy), or the Hallmark God who dwells in fluffy clouds with Santa Claus and the Easter Bunny knew they would be the perfect parents for this precious little angel, because they are so strong and wise and good. Baloney. Parents of kids with special needs are just normal people parenting under extreme circumstances. Some are good parents, some are great, some are bad parents, and some are horrible. Let it be what it is.

DON'T JUDGE THE KIDS

For the love of all that is good and holy, don't treat children with cognitive or neurological differences like they are naughty little terrors. Don't act surprised when the hearing-impaired kid is always up in everyone's face, or the visually impaired kid won't stop poking at herself. If we could crawl inside their brains for a few hours and experience the world as they do, I think we'd have a lot more empathy. Since we can't do the Vulcan mind meld, let's just choose to err on the side of grace and compassion.

MAKE A PLAN

If you are involved in children's ministries at your church, schedule a time to sit down with the parents of children with special needs and make a plan. What does the child need to function well and feel safe? Are there certain things that set her off? Certain strategies that work well at home and could be employed at the church? How can you partner with the family to make church a positive experience for the child, and for them?

INVEST IN ADAPTIVE GEAR

Picture schedules, chunky adaptive crayons, noise-canceling headphones, and pop-up tents and tunnels that create cozy enclosed spaces can go a long way toward helping kids with special needs feel comfortable. A small weighted blanket for a kid to snuggle up in when they're stressed would be a nice thing to keep on hand—if there is a quilting group in your church, they'd probably love the challenge of making one. And what kid isn't captivated by bottles filled with glittering gel? (Google "calm down jars." They're awesome. Just make sure, if you make your own, that you use plastic and glue the lid on.) Adaptive gear can make a world of difference for kids with special needs.

STAFF FOR SUCCESS

One of the best things your church can do for kids with special needs (and for all kids, actually) is to have the same well-trained person in the nursery every week. All children thrive on having a consistent caregiver, but it is especially crucial for kids with special needs, who don't deal well with change and need caregivers who are aware of their needs. Hiring someone with a background in early childhood or special education to fill this role is an investment your church won't regret. If that is not possible, make sure that someone in your congregation who is knowledgeable about working with kids with special needs (aside from the children's parents, who need a chance to rest and worship), such as a teacher, speech therapist, or veteran special needs parent, is "on call" to help with any issues that may arise. A cell phone set to vibrate is an easy way to call people out of the service if they are needed.

LET IT BE DIFFICULT

Making space for people with special needs and ministering to them well can be difficult. And that is okay. Just because something is difficult doesn't mean it's not good. Just because you don't see the results you long for doesn't mean it's not worth doing. Welcome to the realities of loving someone with special needs. Stay the course. Let it be difficult, and do it anyway.

Throw a Shower

You know what church ladies are traditionally really good at? (Of course you do, but I'm going to say it anyway.) Throwing showers. The women at my home church had it down to a science: cake, punch, crepe-paper decorations, and corny party games. If I close my eyes, I can still smell the party mints and peanuts. (I am not sure who came up with the idea of ruining those two perfectly nice foods by mixing them together, but I forgive them.)

Party mints and peanuts aside, showers are a lot of fun. Who doesn't love the chance to get together with their girlfriends, eat, and gossip about babies and weddings? Who doesn't love swooning over tiny little baby booties, or oohing and aahing over someone's cushy new towel set? If you invite every woman in the church, as my church always did, showers are a great way for ladies to get to know each other, especially across generational lines. And throwing showers for newcomers, single moms, and anyone from the community who needs a little love is a great way to show we care and invite them deeper into community.

Even if there aren't any weddings or new babies on the horizon, you can still throw a shower. Contact the local women's shelter or crisis pregnancy center and see what they need. Of course, cash donations are always welcome, but many of these places pass out diapers, formula, and baby blankets like they're party mints and peanuts. And women transitioning out of shelters need the same things new brides do to establish their households: towels, toasters, bedding, can openers, and enough cookware to fry an egg or boil pasta. Throwing a shower is a fun way to meet those needs, and bonus: it creates an opportunity to highlight these vital local ministries and discuss more ways the women at your church can be involved. Invite a representative from the shelter or center; they may or may not be able to come (don't be offended if they can't), but if they can, they can give you the inside scoop, and maybe haul the loot away too.

Finally, can I make a humble suggestion? Work with the older ladies on this one. Showers used to be a much bigger deal than they are today, and the sixty- and seventy-somethings might get really excited about the chance to work with you on the planning. Goodness knows there are few people in our youth-obsessed society who ask for their opinion and value what they have to say. I know, I know; you may have a Pinterest-worthy vision of burlap, chalkboards, and paleo-diet nibbles. But let the nice ladies have their crepe paper, cut-glass dishes, and party mints and peanuts. Who says you can't have both? Flex and flow, friends. It's just a shower, and relationships are infinitely more precious than party decorations.

Start an Evening Bible Study

I'm a big fan of morning Bible studies. They are a great option for stay-at-home moms with kids who still need afternoon naps, and for retirees who don't like to drive at night. I attended them for years when my children were young. But oh, church. If there is one surefire way to isolate women who work full time, to make sure all the single moms and career women know that we don't care about their needs and have no interest in investing in their spiritual growth until they quit their jobs and become Suzy Homemaker, it is to schedule all the events for women during the day, when they can't come.

Seriously, church. What are you thinking? Knock it off.

I'm usually not a big fan of doing something just for the sake of doing it, but if you have a morning Bible study for women, you should have an evening one too. One with childcare, because not every woman has a reliable partner she can leave her kids home with. I don't even care if no one comes to the study at first, or if they don't bring their kids; just having the option available shows that you value *all* the women in your church, no matter how they spend their days.

It doesn't even have to be an evening study; you could take a cue from men's groups and meet early in the morning or over lunch downtown. You could group moms and kids together in someone's living room, or hold a big to-do in the church sanctuary. You could do a video series, or have your pastor or another gifted woman get up and teach, or just read and discuss the Bible together. You could do it book-club style, choosing one Christian book to read each month and then getting together for hors d'oeuvres and conversation. Do whatever works for the women in your church, but for the love of working women, do something. Make sure all the women in your church know they are wanted, valued, and welcome to participate.

Get Governmental

I attended my first church business meeting when I was nineteen years old. I was not impressed. My husband, Aaron, had accepted a worship leader position at a local church a few days before our wedding, making me a pastor's wife before I was even out of my teens. For the most part, it was a great fit. I loved the people, I loved the church, and they were incredibly gracious with the young kids they had hired to breathe new life into their music program. But the church business meetings? I couldn't understand why they insisted on "making motions" and "seconding" everything, how they could debate the wording of a clause for fifteen minutes, or why anyone cared so much about the color of the church carpeting. It seemed pretentious—an aggravating waste of time spent on details that didn't really matter.

My feelings about church meetings haven't changed much over the past twenty years. I still feel like heaving an adolescent sigh of impatience when we get hung up on details, and I don't think I have ever forced the words "so moved" past my lips. But my attitude *has* changed. As annoying and pretentious and flat-out boring as church governance can be, it is an integral part of running a church faithfully, responsibly, and well. Somebody needs to make sure that the budget is balanced, the roof isn't in danger of collapsing on the congregants, and we have good safety protocols in place to screen the people who work with our children. And in all but the most staff-led churches, these meetings are also the place where the vision of the church is discussed, new initiatives are voted on, and the trajectory of the church is set.

In short, you should be there. No fair complaining about everything that's wrong with your church if you won't attend the meetings where they discuss and vote on such things. Maybe if more young people got involved in church governance, instead of being all Peter Pan about it, we would begin to see more widespread, institutional change.

Different churches function in different ways. Deacons, elders, councils, boards; you may need to do a little research to figure out how your church is run, if you don't already know. My home church used a council system: different ministries within the church were run by their own councils, and the chair of each council sat on the church council, which made broader decisions about the directions of the church. We also had elders who committed to looking after people's spiritual needs, and deacons who committed to looking after people's physical needs. By contrast, the church I am serving at now is run by one board that makes suggestions to the congregation. It is more streamlined, and there are fewer meetings, but the bulk of the work falls on a smaller core of people. There are pluses and minuses to every form of governance, and none of them are really more biblical than the others, even if they give people scriptural sounding titles like "elder" or "deacon." What is biblical is working together in a spirit of cooperation to build up Christ's church and steward the spiritual, human, and material resources it has been entrusted with.

Is it time for you to get governmental?

Form a Collective

When I was a teenager, my grandma, two aunts, and a close family friend had a "honey do" collective. They'd spend one afternoon per week at a member's house to tackle the project of her choice: painting guest rooms, organizing closets, framing and hanging family photos, catching up on dirty dishes and unfolded laundry—whatever. The next week, it would be the next woman's turn. As you can probably imagine, they got a ton done and had a blast doing it. The kids would play together while the women worked, but if they needed attention, one of the women (usually grandma) would leave the other three to their work while she bandaged boo-boos, broke up fights, and doled out Kool-Aid.

It was amazing.

Imagine this. What if instead of recoiling in horror when a friend's five-year-old is diagnosed with leukemia, we invaded her house with vacuums and toilet brushes every time he had chemo? What if instead of assuring that single mom of our prayers, we assured her of our willingness to babysit? What if, instead of each one of us struggling along in isolation, we banded together and *really* took care of one other? What if we let each other into our messy lives so that we could give and receive blessings we cut ourselves off from otherwise?

What if the church *actually* functioned like family?

What an incredible witness that would be to a lonely, fragmented world longing for community. What a lifesaver that would be for those among us who desperately need help, but don't know how to ask for it.

Give this a try with a couple friends from church. Maybe you could start with a babysitting collective, so each of you has one kid-free evening per month. Maybe you could take turns whipping up tasty meals and dropping them off at each other's houses. Maybe you could have basement-purging parties every so often. Maybe Allison could change everyone's oil, and Miriam could prep everyone's lawn for the next season, and Sarah could organize everyone's cupboards on a quarterly basis. Whatever works, and blesses each member of your little group. Be creative.

Some churches do a similar thing on a larger scale. People volunteer their time or expertise, either as a service to other church members or in exchange for other people's services. Of course, you can do a straight-up trade—you fix my car, I paint your kid's bedroom. But some churches use a credit system to make it more flexible and accessible. Joe fixes Grandma Betty's sink, Grandma Betty bakes ten pies for Armida's Thanksgiving bash, Armida shuttles Joe's kids from school to dance class on Thursdays during the month he's stuck on overtime. It's a bit transactional, but it's still a great way to build connections and to begin to function as an organic, interdependent community committed to serving one another.

Don't Let Anyone Leave Hungry

Did you know that potlucks are one of the earliest church rituals? Once upon a time, communion didn't consist of a bite of bread and a sip of Welch's. No, the early church's love feasts were real feasts, a celebration of the abundance Jesus fed us with through his life, death, and resurrection. And the party wasn't limited to Sundays, either. Acts 2:42–47 gives us one of the best descriptions of church ever: "They devoted themselves to the apostles' teaching and to fellowship, to the breaking of bread and to prayer. Everyone was filled with awe at the many wonders and signs performed by the apostles. All the believers were together and had everything in common. They sold property and possessions to give to anyone who had need. Every day they continued to meet together in the temple courts. They broke bread in their homes and ate together with glad and sincere hearts, praising God and enjoying the favor of all the people. And the Lord added to their number daily those who were being saved."

I mean, yeah! Who wouldn't want to be part of that?

Most of our churches come up short in the "wonders and signs" department, and even our best preachers lack the immediacy of Peter and his buddies. But ladies? We can pull off the food part. We might even be able to do it with glad and sincere hearts. And I wouldn't be at all surprised if the Lord added to our number daily those who are being saved.

Fifteen percent of Americans, and more than 20 percent of American children, live in food-insecure households.[1] This doesn't mean that they have nothing to eat; in fact, people living in poverty have a much higher risk of obesity. Food insecurity means that families buy the cheapest food available, regardless of its nutritional value; that eighty-seven-year-old widows have to choose between running their air-conditioning and buying the eggs and tuna fish they rely on for protein; that kids may miss out on healthy meals over the weekend or during the summer, when they're not in school to receive free breakfasts and lunches. Ramen, mac and cheese, and cheap potato chips are easy and inexpensive ways to fill rumbling tummies, but they're not exactly healthy. They don't exactly nourish hungry bodies, minds, and hearts.

We can do so much better.

There are many ways your church can engage with hunger in your community. Do regular collection drives for your local food pantry, reminding your people that man does not live on canned yams alone. Consider hosting a food pantry or salvaged food distribution site at your own church—it's a great way to get people through the doors. Get a few of your domestic geniuses together to come up with a month's worth of healthy, inexpensive freezer meals, do some wheeling and dealing with the manager of a nearby grocery store to get the goods you need on the cheap, and invite folks to pile into the church on a Saturday to prep thirty days of dinners for a nominal fee. Pack healthy lunches and deliver them to area schools on Fridays, to be sent home with vulnerable kids over the weekend. Put on a giant potluck after church every Sunday, and invite the entire community to attend.

The early church expressed the love of God, and their love for one another, through food. So can we. Let's get cooking, ladies!

234

Because They Said So!

Bright Ideas from Mentor Moms

Write notes! If your church has a mailbox system, write a quick, encouraging note to one person per week, and pop it in their mailbox. Everyone needs a little encouragement, and a note letting them know that they are seen and appreciated could make their day, if not their year.
—Jenny Rae Armstrong, mama of four

Each of our small groups at church adopts a local mission to support during their semester-long Bible study. We've served meals at the local women's shelter, cleaned up a school garden, took over a Laundromat for a few hours to offer free laundry and soap, volunteered at a citywide recycling drive, and more. The group selects the mission together, and often the whole church is invited to come along.
—Erin F. Wasinger, mama of three

Buy a frozen lasagna. I hate cooking, and fail at all domestic tasks. Yet I'm committed to building community to the glory of God. So instead of feeling the pressure to cook a fancy meal, I head to the freezer section and buy a lasagna.
—Catherine McNiel, mama of three

Connect long-term with one of your church's international mission partners. Learn about their country and the unique challenges of their ministry. If and when the Lord prompts, travel and serve alongside them in country to help further their ministry and outreach.
—Sharon R. Hoover, mama of two

Talk to the older ladies in church. I don't mean the fifty-something moms with trendy clothes and perfectly applied cosmetics (although you should talk to them too)—I mean the spiral-permed saints who hobble in with their walkers. Old ladies are all but invisible in our society, treated as irrelevant at best and irritating at worst. It's disgusting. Be countercultural, and make a point to chat with the older ladies before and after services, getting to know them and letting them get to know you.

    —Jenny Rae Armstrong, mama of four

Comparison kills spiritual growth! I learned this after years of struggling to grow with little ones at home. Don't compare yourself with moms who might not have a similar situation to you or may be in a very different season of life. Also, don't compare where you are now with where you used to be spiritually. Your development will change in this season you are in.

    —Nicole T. Walters, mama of two

Organize a summer day camp for refugee children in the nearest low-income housing complex, or tutor their moms in English. You will have an immediate inroad with the family, and be blessed with unique cuisine (like cassava leaf stew!) in return.

    —Margaret Philbrick, mama of three

For those of you moms with little ones with newly discovered special needs, you are not meant to carry it all on your own. Ask for help. Trust that those who respond consider it an honor and a privilege to come alongside you. Don't waste your precious energy comparing yourself to other moms, but instead receive the grace God wants to give you—in spades.

    —Carrie Kuba, mama of a lovely Habesha from Ethiopia
      and a medically fragile daughter

Notes

[1] "Hunger and Poverty Fact Sheet," *Feeding America,* www.feedingamerica.org/hunger-in-america/impact-of-hunger/hunger-and-poverty/hunger-and-poverty-fact-sheet.html (accessed October 19, 2015).

AFTERWORD

There's nothing like writing a book about things moms can do to change the world to make you examine your own life. Writing this book has challenged me, and not just in the I-have-four-kids-and-a-job-and-I'm-doing-WHAT? sense. It has challenged me in the please-God-don't-let-me-be-a-raging-hypocrite sense. It has also inspired me, especially as I've learned how other moms are impacting their world for Christ. Since starting this project, I've found myself shopping less and giving more. I say yes to my kids' requests to have friends over more often. I try to pay attention to the way I look at people when I'm out and about; whether my gaze affirms their dignity or makes them feel dismissed or judged. And yes, I am still sporting my natural dark "blahnd" hair (for now, at least). I hope that this book has challenged and inspired you as well; that you have found a couple takeaways that have blessed you and helped you bless those around you.

If there is one thing that I want to leave you with, it is that verse from 2 Timothy 1:6–7. "For this reason I remind you to fan into flame the gift of God, which is in you through the laying on of my hands. For the Spirit God gave us does not make us timid, but gives us power, love and self-discipline." Beloved sisters, I am laying hands on my computer as I pray this prayer over you. I imagine my hands joining the hands of every woman who has